RDON UNIVERSITY

eturn this book

Yo

Dress, Body, Culture

Series Editor **Joanne B. Eicher**, *Regents' Professor, University of Minnesota*

Books in this provocative series seek to articulate the connections between culture and dress which is defined here in its broadest possible sense as any modification or supplement to the body. Interdisciplinary in approach, the series highlights the dialogue between identity and dress, cosmetics, coiffure, and body alterations as manifested in practices as varied as plastic surgery, tattooing, and ritual scarification. The series aims, in particular, to analyze the meaning of dress in relation to popular culture and gender issues and will include works grounded in anthropology, sociology, history, art history, literature, and folklore.

ISSN: 1360-466X

DRESS, BODY, CULTURE

Orlan

Millennial Female

Kate Ince

BERG

Oxford • New York

First published in 2000 by
Berg
Editorial offices:
150 Cowley Road, Oxford, OX4 1JJ, UK
838 Broadway, Third Floor, New York, NY 10003-4812, USA

Berg is an imprint of Oxford International Publishers Ltd.

Library of Congress Cataloging-in-Publication Data
A catalogue record for this book is available from the Library of Congress.

British Library Cataloguing-in-Publication Data
A catalogue record for this book is available from the British Library.

ISBN   1 85973 334 4 (Cloth)
          1 85973 339 5 (Paper)

Typeset by JS Typesetting, Wellingborough, Northants.
Printed in the United Kingdom by Biddles Ltd, Guildford and King's Lynn.

I dedicate this book to the memory of my father,
Walter N. Ince.

Contents

Acknowledgements

This book has been several years in the making, and I would like to thank a number of people and organizations. Firstly The British Academy for awarding me a grant for a visit to Paris in 1996 that got research started, and secondly the School of Humanities of the University of Birmingham, for partly funding my visit to Paris to meet and interview Orlan in August 1998. Librarians in the Bibliothèque Forney and the Bibliothèque Marguerite Durand in Paris were always patient and helpful, as they were in the British Library in London. I am grateful to the organizers of several conferences where early ideas and work-in-progress were presented: 'Feminism and the Aesthetics of Difference' (Institute of Romance Studies, London, September 1995), 'Considered Unsightly: a Transdisciplinary Conference on the Freakish and the Monstrous' (Centre for Cultural Studies, University of Leeds, October 1997), and the annual conference of the Society for French Studies (University of Edinburgh, March 1999).

A number of friends and colleagues have extended invitations to me to present papers on Orlan in their departments and institutions while I have been preparing this book, and I would especially like to thank Diane Morgan (then at Teesside), Victoria Best (Cambridge), Avril Horner and Ursula Tidd (Salford), and Nicola Bown (Birmingham) for so doing. Thanks also to Martin Halliwell and Nicholas Zurbrugg of De Montfort University for accepting my offer to respond to Orlan's presentation at the conference 'Rethinking the Avant-garde' in Leicester in October 1998. For their advice about particular research leads I am particularly endebted to Céline Surprenant and Emma Wilson, and for their kind assistance with information and materials I would like to thank Sarah Wilson and Duncan McCorquodale. My more personal thanks for their interest, support, encouragement and friendship at different times during the book's composition go to Douglas Smith, Carolyn Burdett, Ian James, Dennis Wood, Jens Roehrkasten, and Christine Everley, and my especial gratitude to Christine for all the newspaper cuttings. Personal acknowledgements would not be complete without mentioning Lewis Johnson, who didn't actually help, but without whom the book might never have been written.

Material from this study has appeared in two other publications, and I am grateful to Victoria Best and Peter Collier for allowing the reprinting, in modified form, of the article 'Between the Acts' that appears in *Powerful Bodies: Performance in French Cultural Studie*s (Peter Lang, 1999). An earlier, shorter version of Chapter 1 'Operations of Redress: Orlan, the body, and its limits' appeared in Issue 2 no 2 of *Fashion Theory* (1998), and I would like to thank Valerie Steele and Kathryn Earle for previewing my work in that excellent journal. I would also particularly like to thank Kathryn Earle for commissioning this study in the first place, and for her patience and sound advice throughout the time it has taken me to write it. Lastly but most of all, I want to thank Orlan for her hospitality, kindness and generosity with materials when I met her in 1998, for her friendliness and helpfulness in all subsequent communications, and for allowing me to reprint the illustrations of her performances and other works listed below.

List of Illustrations

1. 'One-off strip-tease with trousseau sheets', Espace Lyonnais d'Art Contemporain, 1976, 1.75 × 1.35m. In the collection of the Nouveau Musée of Villeurbanne.
2. 'White Madonna in Assumption' on video monitor and clouds of bubble wrap, 1984. Cibachrome, 110cm × 165cm. Photo by ACE3P photo school.
3. 'Imaginary credits no. 15', title of the virtual (unmade) film 'For all miracles, consult our tarifs'. Painted cinema poster, acrylic on canvas, 200cm × 300cm, 1986. Photo by Joël Nicolas.
4. 'Black virgin and video', 1984. Cibachrome on aluminium, 120 × 175 cm. Photo by Jean-Paul Lefert for the ACE3P photo school, Ivry-sur-Seine.
5. 'Measuring' performance in the Piazza S. Pietro of the Vatican, Rome, 1974. Photo by Jean-Luc Waumann.
6. Street measuring, 1978; final pose of action by the Orlan-body, holding up relic of dirty water from dress washed in public. Black and white photo, 110cm × 165cm.
7. Close-up in red, blue and green on the opening of the body during the 7th operation-performance 'Omnipresence', New York, 21 November 1993. Cibachrome in diasec vacuum, 165cm × 110cm. Photo by Vladimir Sichov for SIPA Press.
8. 'The second mouth', 7th operation-performance 'Omnipresence', New York, 21 November 1993. Cibachrome in diasec vacuum, 165cm × 110cm. Photo by Vladimir Sichov for SIPA Press.
9. 3 relics 'this is my body this is my software', 'I gave my body to art', 'happening in the operating theatre', soldered metal and burglarproof glass, 10g of my flesh encased in resin, 30cm × 30cm × 5cm, 1993.
10. Finger drawing in blood, done during the eighth surgical intervention, 1993. 100cm × 70cm.
11. Carnal art 'detachment' ('décollement', of face) during the 7th operation-performance 'Omnipresence', New York, 21 November 1993. Cibachrome in diasec vacuum, 165cm × 110cm. Photo by Vladimir Sichov for SIPA Press.

Author's Note

Throughout this book I have used the Harvard author-date system of giving references, in order to keep notes to a minimum. All publications referred to in this way in the main text are listed in the bibliography. Where translations of French material are available and have been referred to, details are given in the bibliography; otherwise, all translations from the French are my own.

Introduction: The Story of Orlan

Orlan is a French multimedia and performance artist whose performances over the last decade have consisted of cosmetic surgery. In 1990 she took the term 'operating theatre' literally and embarked on a project entitled 'The Reincarnation of Saint Orlan', which has consisted of performing – remaining conscious throughout, photographing, filming and broadcasting – a series of operations to totally remodel her face and body, and thus her identity.

The fact that 'Orlan' is not the artist's 'real' name, but one she gave herself at the age of fifteen in 1962, is one indication of how pivotal the question of identity has been to Orlan's career. While sounding to some like a man's name (Lemoine-Luccioni 1983: 140), it fairly bubbles with polysemous and suggestive cultural connotations; 'Orlan-do' the sex-changing hero(ine) of Virginia Woolf's famous novel, Orlon the synthetic fibre, and the glossily advertised perfume Orlane. When just the name's initial letter 'O' is taken, it is perhaps even more suggestively connotative: the 'O' of 'Other', the 'O' of Pauline Réage's infamous erotic – or pornographic – novel *Story of O/Histoire d'O*, the 'O' that signifies and figures the opening of all orifices. Orlan's story of how she 'found' her name and rebaptized herself points to another of its elements, the poetic, polysemous and psychoanalytically overdetermined syllable 'or' (= gold):

> I decided to change my name completely, to begin with because I was doing some acting and also because I was in a conservatoire when you got thrown out if you used your own name for acting purposes. It grew little by little, then I decided to have psychoanalysis. At the third session the only thing the analyst said to me was: "The next time you'll pay me in cash, not by cheque", whereas I had been paying by cheque. Just as I was signing the last cheque he said "no, on second thoughts, carry on paying by cheque". Since these were the only words he'd uttered in the whole session, this contradictory message was very perturbing. I tried to work out what had gone on in the session, but I couldn't. At the next session [. . .] as I was signing the cheque, I realized that I was signing, in very clear, precise, childlike writing, with a name which wasn't mine [. . . from the most beautifully

written signatures] I had chosen the style of the one in which "dead' [*morte*] was clearly readable. So, as I was deciding not to be dead any more, I used just the positive syllable from the word, the letters O R.[1]

Another famous name connoted by Orlan's is of course that of France's Saint Joan of Arc, the Maid of *Orléans*. Orlan's Frenchness is an issue few commentators have seemed willing to venture an opinion of, and it has even been suggested that the kind of artistic work she does is atypically French (Savary 1998: 119). This remark was in fact made about a stage of Orlan's career one might be tempted to characterize as more 'French' than much of it, the 'sensual, mystical and baroque' performances and installations of the 1980s (ibid.). It was in 1971 that Orlan adopted the persona of Saint Orlan, and much of her work of the 1970s and 1980s drew extensively on biblical and Catholic personae and on other religious iconography, and was set up in churches. The attitudes to institutional religion struck in these installations and performances – from ornate pastiche to pointedly disrespectful parody – tapped and exploited a rich source, the conflict-ridden store of imagery in Catholic art history in which sexuality and religion coincide. Religious imagery has also abounded in the staging of Orlan's operations, and it is difficult to ignore the parallel between religious martyrdom and the suffering (although Orlan argues it otherwise) inflicted by surgery undergone for aesthetic reasons. As Sarah Wilson has observed, making the link between this aspect of Orlan's work and her identity as French, 'it is in a former Catholic country that Orlan has undertaken the sacrilegious task of managing her own metamorphosis, her refiguration and her transsexualism from woman to woman: "This woman tells us that the madonna is a transvestite/female impersonator"' (Wilson 1995: 302). But the issue of Orlan's national identity, and the French context out of which her extensive body of work has arisen, has not so far been discussed in any detail, and for this reason I would like to explore it here, as a prelude to and non-determining context for the readings of her work that follow.

Thanks to the research and scholarship of numerous feminist critics, many of them British or American rather than French, and most of them female, the context(s) of production of French women's writing since 1968 are now well documented. The May 1968 *événements* provided the impetus for the wide-ranging and enormously fertile wave of women's cultural production seen in France in the 1970s, a wave supported and provoked by feminist political groupings such as the *MLF* (*Mouvement de Libération des Femmes*)

---

1. 'Signalement d'Orlan', interview with Maurice Mallet for VST, VST 23-4 sept–déc 1991, 14–15, p. 15.

that were created from 1968 onwards. Although this outburst of feminist thought, writing and other cultural activity died away in France after 1981, its value and interest for women's culture and self-advancement internationally was sustained into the 1980s and well beyond by landmark publications such as Elaine Marks and Isabelle de Courtviron's *New French Feminisms* (1981) and Toril Moi's *French Feminist Thought* (1987). Edited anthologies like these, along with a quantity of other publications on individual authors and theorists too numerous to mention, came to constitute the discursive phenomenon known as 'French feminism', a phenomenon that continued to fuel feminist research all over the globe as the twentieth century drew to its close.

However, although French women's writing – literary and theoretical – has had such an enormous impact on international feminism since the late 1960s, the same cannot really be said of the work of French women visual artists. In the 1970s there were certainly groups and collectives in France to which women painters, photographers and multimedia artists belonged, such as 'Spirale' founded by writer Catherine Valabrègue in 1972 to study 'smothered creativity' (*la création étouffée*), and the association of feminist actresses and film-makers 'Musidora', founded in October 1973 (Marks and de Courtviron 1981: 25). An excerpt by film-maker Viviane Forrester from a volume of essays written by members of 'Musidora' and published by the feminist publishing house *des femmes* in 1976 (*Paroles . . . elles tournent*) is included in *New French Feminisms*, and puts some of the central questions that must have preoccupied French women visual artists of the time:

We don't know what women's vision is. What do women's eyes see? [. . .] I don't know. [. . .] I only know what men's eyes see./ So what do men's eyes see? A crippled world, mutilated, deprived of women's vision. In fact men share our malaise, suffer from the same tragedy: the absence of women [. . .]/ How can male directors today not beg women to pick up the camera, to open up unknown areas to them, to liberate them from their redundant vision which is deeply deformed by this lack? Women's vision is what is lacking and this lack not only creates a vacuum but it perverts, alters, annuls every statement. (Marks and de Courtviron 1981: 181–2)

Events and publications from the 1970s that were specific to women visual artists can be traced; in June 1975 the feminist journal *Les Cahiers du GRIF* devoted an issue to the broad topic of 'creation' that included articles on and by women artists, and the March 1977 issue of *Art Press International* was entitled 'Femmes-Différences', and featured writings on painters and performance artists, as well as an article about women's struggle to find a place in male-dominated art history. Also in 1977, the French feminist journal *Sorcières* produced a number called 'L'Art et les femmes' that contains a substantial dossier of short writings by artists such as Michèle Katz and Léa Lublin, and another dossier of reproductions of paintings, drawings and photographs by these and many other women artists.[2] In general, though, the extensive critical discourse that grew up around women's literary production in France in the 1970s seems not to extend to women's visual art practice. From the late 1970s on, the academic and art critic Aline Dallier published articles on the women's movement in art in which she describes how research and the production of discourse on women artists was lagging behind parallel work on women writers, and in 1982 she organized a conference in Toulouse called 'Le mouvement des femmes dans l'art', in the proceedings of which she states that in 1982, to her knowledge, the University of Paris VIII (Saint-Denis) was the only French university offering a module in women's art.[3] Library catalogues in France turn up only a tiny number of publications relating to French women's art practice, the vast majority of relevant publications being in English, or Italian. Although the issues relevant to French women's artistic production, such as their place in the 'canon' of art history and the production and dissemination of criticism about their work, were being considered by their literary counterparts, women's visual art practice in France in the 1970s seems never to have gained the discursive support it needed to support and foster its practitioners.

Essential to the dissemination of all work in the visual arts is the organization of exhibitions and other events at which works can be viewed, and as with the paucity of relevant critical discourse, there seem to have been very few events in France after 1968 that focused particularly or exclusively on women's art. An exception was an exhibition called 'Women's role in contemporary art' ('La Part des femmes dans l'art contemporain') which took place at the municipal Arts Centre in Vitry-sur-Seine, just outside the city of Paris, in 1984, and which received funding from the French Ministry of Culture as well as from the short-lived Ministry of Women's Rights that had been founded several years before. The catalogue to this exhibition consists of short descriptions of the work of some ninety-four contemporary women artists, mostly painters, many of them living and working in Paris, although a striking number were born in countries other than France. Prefaced by Yvette Roudy, then Minister for Women's Rights in France, the catalogue reveals that despite State funding, the exhibition's budget did not stretch to the technical support needed to show video art or certain other types of installation or performance, or to the borrowing of 'essential' works from

2. *Sorcières* no. 10 (July 1977), 'L'Art et les femmes', eds Xavière Gauthier and Anne Rivière.
3. Aline Dallier-Poppier, 'La recherche universitaire sur l'art des femmes', A 13 (71) in proceedings of conference 'Le mouvement des femmes dans l'art' (Colloque National Femmes, Féminisme, Recherches), University of Toulouse, 1982.

other European countries or America. In addition, an introduction to the catalogue by the Deputy Mayor of Vitry-sur-Seine is highly revealing about the attitude of the French State to feminism in 1984, three years after the return of a socialist government to power but more than a decade after the initial wave of post-1968 feminist activity; Jean Collet says of the women-only exhibition:

> Of course, for us this is not a question of any kind of 'feminist' demonstration. We are not seeking to illustrate any specifically feminine approach to artistic creation, in opposition to a definably masculine approach. The fear that some people have expressed about a reverse 'neo-sexism' is not relevant here, and we are not getting involved in any derisory conflict of women against men.[4]

A second introduction to the exhibition, also written by a man and evidently just as conscious of the female specificity already built into the organization of the event, speaks of the necessity of avoiding the creation of an 'artistic ghetto' that would serve the aims of the feminist movement. '[W]ithout neglecting the political necessities of the feminist struggle, we see in these women painters and sculptors who, like men, are affirming their identity as artists in today's art and today's society, not in some secondary or marginal category' (ibid.: 8). Women's art and culture constitutes a 'secondary' domain, and feminism is only ever going to reinforce cultural ghettoization; these comments are all too typical of the incapacity to deal with the issue of women's cultural specificity that continued – and continues – to dog official discourse in France after the momentous events of the 1970s.

Since 1984, the climate of women's visual art practice in France has continued to be less positive and less dynamic than in other European countries or in the United States, for the same reasons as are revealed by attitudes to the 1984 Vitry-sur-Seine exhibition. Fewer events and exhibitions are organized, fewer books and articles are published, and women artists working in France continue to depend to a considerable extent on the support of their fellow-practitioners abroad. Given the very nature of exchanges and exhibiting in the art world, whose movements have perhaps always operated across national boundaries more than those of the literary world (doubtless in part because they are not language-dependent), and which have certainly been very international since the avant-gardes of the early twentieth century, this is perhaps not too unusual. But as the published proceedings of a 1990 conference at the Ecole nationale supérieure des Beaux-Arts in Paris show,

---

4. Jean Collet, 'Un événement artistique', in 'La part des femmes dans l'art contemporain', catalogue to exhibition held at the Centre d'animation culturelle, Ville de Vitry-sur-Seine, March 1984, p. 5.

women's art in France really does lack a strong nationally-based context. The volume in question, entitled *Féminisme, art et histoire de l'art*, consists principally of translated essays by British and North American feminist art critics, Griselda Pollock and Lisa Tickner amongst them, and its introduction by Yves Michaud, the director of the Ecole nationale supérieure des Beaux-Arts, is devoted almost entirely to the exposition ('translation') of anglophone feminist theory and criticism, and of feminist theories of spectatorship *à la* Laura Mulvey, some fifteen years after 'Visual pleasure and narrative cinema' was first published. To its credit, Michaud's introduction is entirely open about France's failure to absorb and make use of the theoretical work and criticism she has herself produced and inspired (in many cases), and he opens with a lament about the lack of familiarity to be found in France with feminist approaches to artistic production or critical discourse about that production (Michaud 1994: 9).

I shall conclude this introduction by rapidly filling in some important facts about 'The Reincarnation of Saint Orlan', by making a few remarks about the reception of Orlan's work, and by giving an outline of the chapters that constitute the main part of the book.

The first official instalment of Orlan's surgical self-reinvention took place on 30 May 1990. It was the beginning of a planned sequence of operations, each of which was to focus on a specific feature of Orlan's face. There was no *one* model for Orlan's self-remodelling; each feature is surgically resculpted to match a specific feature of a different great icon in the history of Western art: the nose of a famous unattributed School of Fontainebleau sculpture of Diana, the mouth of Boucher's Europa, the forehead of Leonardo's Mona Lisa, the chin of Botticelli's Venus and the eyes of Gérard's Psyche. Pastiche or parody of the fetishistic fragmentation of the female body by male artists is clearly intended, but this plural aesthetic is also a critical-if-imitative repetition of the composition of a beautiful face practised by the Greek painter Zeuxis, who '"when painting his portrait of Helena in the city of Kroton, [chose] five virgins, so as to reproduce the most beautiful part of each one".[5] While this procedure traditionally relates to the image of woman from the man's point of view, which confers on the artist a creative and thus god-like status, Orlan takes it up from the woman's viewpoint before the backdrop of the present' (Ermacora 1994: 16). Orlan also uses the fragmented character of the image she is composing to effect in her operation-performances, where the aesthetic genre of the detail is advertised by the display of reproductions of just the faces of her various icons. An accentuation of this effect is created by the highlighting, on each reproduction, of the feature to be copied.

5. Ernst Kris, Otto Kurz, *Die Legende vom Künstler. Ein geschichtlicher Versuch*, Frankfurt am Main: Suhrkamp, 1980, p. 68, quoted in Ermacora 1994: 16.

It is surely because she is working with – and in – the flesh that Orlan's surgical project has brought her such attention (not to say notoriety) in the press, both academic and popular. Performance art is generically inclined to attract attention; to quote from the French literary theorist Gérard Genette, performance art might be defined as 'any human activity whose perception is in itself capable of producing and organising an immediate aesthetic effect' (Genette 1994: 66).[6] Orlan therefore has the medium on her side, but nevertheless adds much to this basic effect-producing orientation of 'live' art. All her operations, but most strikingly 'Omnipresence', the seventh and most extensively filmed operation-performance, have involved the use of quasi-theatrical sets, costumes, and multiple media, while also offering representational complexity and a degree of staginess which borders on camp. Orlan's exhibition of surgery involves a display of gore which exercises much the same fascination as medical documentaries, whilst also capitalizing on the dramatic potential of the operating theatre exploited by television hospital series. Her work almost invariably produces an effect in, and a reaction from, those who learn of it. To what extent it is actual images of the flesh which produce that effect, and to what extent the 'Reincarnation' project is conceptual – in other words, it is the idea of what Orlan is doing that strikes the receiver rather than the actual images and objects produced – is a fascinating question, and one about which readers of this book are bound to have different views.

This study of Orlan's 35-year career as a multimedia and performance artist is organized thematically rather than chronologically. Although Chapter 1 concentrates just on early works, and on performances that precede 1990 and 'The Reincarnation of Saint Orlan', Orlan's surgical project is discussed under different heads in all the other chapters, and is the exclusive subject of Chapter 4. 'Reincarnation' is the major artistic project Orlan has undertaken in the 1990s, but not the only one, and in Chapter 3 I also discuss her Mexico-based exploration of standards of beauty in pre-Colombian civilizations, a touring exhibition on which she started work in the mid-1990s. (The digitally produced photographic prints from this project have toured Latin America, the US, and have recently begun to show in Europe.)

One of the most striking qualities of Orlan's work is the breadth of the critical reception it has elicited across the entire spectrum of disciplines, from the visual arts to medicine, and from gender studies to philosophies of ethics. The range of theorists and critics I draw upon in the four chapters of this book are a further reminder of this remarkable breadth of appeal. In Chapter 1,

---

6. 'toute activité humaine dont la perception est en elle-même susceptible de produire et d'organiser (entre autres) un effet esthétique immédiat'.

which treats issues of materials, dress and fashion raised by Orlan's art, especial attention is paid to psychoanalytic readings of dress and the body, and particularly to the response to Orlan's early works made by the Lacanian psychoanalyst Eugénie Lemoine-Luccioni. The last part of the chapter, in which I try to construct a feminist interpretation of the 'mesurages' or body-measurings Orlan performed in public spaces in the late 1960s and 1970s, turns to theories of the imaginary put forward by feminist philosophers Luce Irigaray and Christine Battersby. In Chapter 2, which is devoted mainly to the questions of spectatorship raised by viewing Orlan's performances, I make use of the challenge to patriarchal theories of the gaze formulated by feminist film theorists Carol Clover and Barbara Creed, in their writings on horror cinema. The subject of Chapter 3 is the importance of technology to Orlan's work, and in addition to the enormously influential writings of feminist historian of science Donna Haraway, I draw there on the theories of monstrosity developed by feminist philosopher Rosi Braidotti and cultural theorist Slavoj Zizek, and on the concept of 'faciality' advanced by theorists Gilles Deleuze and Félix Guattari in *A Thousand Plateaus*. Chapter 4 begins with a discussion of Orlan's place in, and contribution to, debates about postmodernist performance art, and moves on to engage with the hugely important theory of gender performativity formulated by Judith Butler. The influence of Butler's feminist deconstructive approach to issues of gender identity and the body can in fact be felt throughout the book, since it was as part of my engagement with Butler's books *Gender Trouble* and *Bodies that Matter*, ongoing early in 1994, that I first heard of and became interested in Orlan. Chapter 4 concludes with my response to the readings of 'The Reincarnation of Saint Orlan' made by Lacanian feminist Parveen Adams, feminist sociologist of cosmetic surgery Kathy Davis, and philosopher Peggy Zeglin Brand.

As I have shown in my summary above of the post-1960s situation in France in which Orlan's career developed, women's identity and the cultural specificity of their artistic productions quickly became the dominant questions to be addressed. One of the performances with which Orlan disrupted feminist political meetings of the time consisted of her brandishing a placard that read 'JE SUIS UNE HOMME ET UN FEMME'; a reversal of the masculine and feminine pronouns that make up the only, binary coding of nouns offered by the French language (Orlan 1996: 85). An indication of the uncertainty and ambivalence about feminism felt by many well-known women writers and artists of the period, this slogan can also stand as evidence of the strength of Orlan's steadfast commitment, throughout her career, to the question of identity. Her multimedia and performance work has been a consistent and probing investigation of human identity – gender identity, but also cultural, national, personal and bodily identity – in an age where identity has become *the* most important question. It is this I hope to show in the readings of her work that follow.

Operations of Redress: Orlan, the Body, and its Limits

Everything came to me from elsewhere, then?
Probably. And yet, however rhapsodically crafted it is, I put on the text this work
has produced. Let anyone who will explain the paradox; the dress is made of bits
and pieces, and yet I wear it and I say it is mine – because it becomes what I make of
it: a sack, a costume, or just a simple dress. I put it on. (Lemoine-Luccioni 1983: 8)

In this passage from Eugénie Lemoine-Luccioni's psychoanalytic study of
dress *La robe*, textuality is returned to its etymological field of weaving (the
Latin *texere*) and the fabrication of materials; Roland Barthes' reminder of
the origin of this word rings in our ears. But we are reminded too of the
thread that runs the other way, from spinning, weaving and sewing to writing,
the crafting of prose and poetry, and the piecing-together of texts. In this
first chapter I shall discuss those of Orlan's works and performances most
intimately involved with material, dress and clothing. In so doing I shall
focus particularly on the contiguity of dress and textuality, in an effort to
unpick, if you like, the textuality of dress, and to consider a different possible
arrangement of the pieces that mysteriously (as Lemoine-Luccioni notes) make
up the garment.

Addressing Women's Clothing: The Early Works

In the 1960s Orlan embarked upon what was to be a long-lasting series of
works involving the sheets of her trousseau – the fabric her mother had set
aside for her married life. Installations and sculptures using stained trousseau
sheets were exhibited in 1966 and 1967 in Saint-Etienne, in Nice, and at the
Espace Lyonnais d'Art Contemporain, in an echo of the traditional demon-
stration of the loss of a bride's virginity (Orlan was of course not married at
the time). Like later works in the series, these exhibitions may be seen against
the background of Orlan's conflictual relationship with her mother, which

became particularly fraught as her daughter reached the age at which she might have been expected to marry and 'settle down'.[1] Orlan's mother was a housewife, her father a theatre electrician, and she had one sister eight years her senior: in an interview conducted in 1991 she explained that the emotional identifications at work in her family divided it into two 'couples' of her sister and her mother, and herself and her father, and that her mother was a typical rather neurotic housewife always preoccupied with her own health and that of her family:

> We were always very distant [. . .] I had to tell her "I'm ill" before she'd start to take an interest in me. My sister always took the advice. She was always ill and she's *still* always ill. When you phone her, the only thing she can talk about is her illness. It's a normal way of getting oneself noticed, getting oneself loved.[2]

Orlan's distance from her mother took the form of a vehement early rejection of marriage and domesticity probably reinforced by early intimations in France of the women's liberation movement that was to become so important after 1968.

A commentary indicating derision for the institution of marriage is evident in Orlan's decision to turn the very materials intended for the private 'sacrosanct' spaces of her marital home to use in the public and visible arena of an art gallery. (As late as 1991, when she had turned 44, Orlan was declaring herself a 'hardened bachelor-girl' ('célibataire endurcie'),[3] although she has more recently, as is widely known, been happily married to the art historian Stéphane Napoli.) Not long afterwards Orlan issued an invitation to artists and art dealers to supply her with their sperm (the 'paint') for her to use on a canvas made of her trousseau sheets. Here the feminist political impetus fuelled by the 1968 context in which she was working became a challenge to the male-dominated mechanics and economics of the art world. The pointed gendering of art materials in the action – the substance to be manipulated and applied is 'male', while the screen or surface receptive to them is 'female', or a traditionally valued female possession – constituted critical distance from the suggested work, while its reversal of roles implied a critique of performances such as Yves Klein's 'Anthropométries' (1958-60), in which a male artist had employed female bodies as an instrument in

1. E.g. Andy Beckett in 'Suffering for her Art', *Independent on Sunday*, 14 April 1996, pp. 18–21 (p. 21).

2. 'Signalement d'Orlan', interview with Maurice Mallet for *VST*, VST 23-4 sept–déc 1991, 14–15, p. 14.

3. ibid.

the artistic production process (Klein's 'models' were daubed in IKB blue paint and instructed to roll on and against his horizontal and vertical canvasses).

A further work exhibited by Orlan at the atelier Delaroa in Saint-Etienne in 1968, 'Chiaroscuro sewing' ('Couture en clair obscure'), involved locating the traces of sperm on her trousseau fabric using badly done embroidery. While maintaining the gender-parodic spirit of her invitation to the male art world to supply her with its sexual bodily fluids, this work also communicated her unskilled unsuitability for the conventionally feminine and domestic art of embroidery.[4] Perhaps the crowning event in the trousseau series, however, was the 'One-off striptease with trousseau sheets' performed at the atelier Delaroa in Lyon in 1975.[5] Both live action and photographed art work, this performance anticipated Orlan's 1980s work by combining the formal poses and composition of high art with the popular medium of the striptease. Conforming to the conventions of stripping by finishing the action naked, but in a contrivedly modest pose resembling the women of religious portraiture far more than the raunchy dances of strip clubs, Orlan's action assembled contradictions about the act of viewing the female body in a way that anticipated more complex later performances. The questions it posed were evidently feminist in inspiration, a feminism also apparent in Orlan's neat overturning of the intended purpose of the trousseau sheets, which instead of wrapping her into confined marital comfort, were employed as drapes to be removed and discarded. The whole performance was planned, choreographed and executed by Orlan herself in a venue not exploitative of women, at least, not in the sense that spectators had come there for gratification or titillation.

After adopting the persona of Saint Orlan in 1971, Orlan started to perform saintliness by exhibiting and having herself photographed draped in billowing robes made of fabrics such as black vinyl and white leatherette. According to the critic Barbara Rose, the incarnation as Saint Orlan 'focused on the hypocrisy of the way society has traditionally split the female image into madonna and whore' (Rose 1993: 84). Uppermost in Orlan's intentions in creating these elaborate sculpted costumes was, obviously, a play with religious iconography; the figures on which she based the tableaux were Madonnas, in different representations, and Bernini's famous statue of the ecstatic Saint Theresa.

4. A piece of this installation was acquired by the FNAC, the French chain of multimedia stores that has long been a sponsor and supporter of the arts in France.

5. Another work acquired by the FNAC, now in the collection of the Nouveau Musée de Villeurbanne.

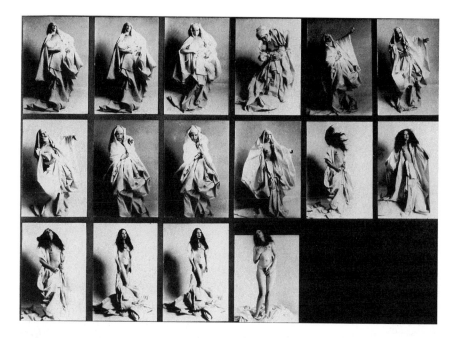

Figure 1. 'One-off strip-tease with trousseau sheets', Espace Lyonnais d'Art Contemporain, 1976, 1.75 × 1.35m. In the collection of the Nouveau Musée of Villeurbanne.

As Rose points out, a strong feminist slant can be detected in the exposure of one breast in the photographs of these tableaux, in the way they ape depictions of the nursing Virgin Mary while also being halfway to a page 3 pin-up. Orlan's trousseau sheets were used again in the series 'The Draping, The Baroque' that started in 1981.[6] The art of Christianity has been an indispensable source, a theme for feminist appropriation, and the focus of sophisticated pastiche in much of Orlan's work of the 1970s and 1980s, and in the next section I shall review the principal works and performances of this period.

Saints and Madonnas in Performance

Orlan's first public performance as a Madonna took place at an international meeting of body artists at the Centre Georges Pompidou, Paris, in 1979, after her arrival at the event enclosed in a chest like an artwork – perhaps an

6. 'The Draping, The Baroque', Palazzo Grassi, Venice, Centre Georges Pompidou, Paris; Halles de Skarbek, Brussels; Pinacothèque, Ravenna; Bologna Theatre; Arc Biennale, Paris. See Orlan 1996, p. 84.

Figure 2. 'White Madonna in Assumption' on video monitor and clouds of bubble wrap, 1984. Cibachrome, 110cm × 165cm. Photo by ACE3P photo school.

allusion to the work of Christo, an artist to whom she often compares herself. Madonnas and the personage of Saint Orlan were the core identities she employed throughout the 1980s; Saint Orlan appeared to bless Lyon's international performance festival in 1983. The most important exhibitions and installations of the decade were the 'Mise en scène for a saint' of 1980, at the Espace d'Art Contemporain in Lyons, the major exhibition 'Skaï et Sky and vidéo' at the J & J Donguy gallery in Paris in 1984, the joint exhibition with Léa Lublin 'Holy Art Histories/Stories' ('Histoires Saintes de l'Art') in Cergy-Pontoise in 1985, and two photographic shows of 1987, one in the architecturally harmonious setting of the Romanesque Abbaye-aux-Dames in Saintes, the other, entitled 'Baroques photographiques', at the Chambre Claire gallery in Paris. Works included in the 1984 'Skaï et Sky and vidéo' exhibition were the photographic and multimedia installations 'Mise en scène for an assumption', and 'The Metaphors of the Sacred', the second of which was also exhibited separately in 1985. Further important works of the 1980s centring on Orlan's sacred personae were the numbered series of so-called documentary studies of *mise-en-scènes* of religious tableaux, and the set of cinema publicity posters for 'virtual' (unmade) films that were exhibited in the 1990 catalogued exhibition '20 years of Saint Orlan's advertising and cinema' ('Les 20 ans de pub et de ciné de Sainte Orlan') in Caen. The tongue-in-cheek slogans on these brightly painted mounted posters included 'Orlan before Saint Orlan', 'Body in Glory' ('Corps en gloire'), 'Saint Orlan Our Lady of Plenty', and 'For all miracles, consult our tarifs'.

In its variety and quantity this 1980s work advanced considerably on the performances and exhibitions of the previous decade. The costumes of Orlan's poses as Saint Orlan, in particular 'The Draping, the Baroque', were folded ornately and magnificently in the manner of baroque statuery, particularly resembling Bernini's white marble. Photography was the main medium of these works, but Orlan also made use of *tableaux vivants* which emphasized that this was a living saint, capable nonetheless of a saint's powers of transformation and self-transformation. 'I am shattering the shell, shattering the marble, breaking open the drapes, and really proposing a new image disconnected from the roots in which I gave birth to myself' (Orlan, quoted in Fabre 1984, p. 5). As Sarah Wilson points out, Orlan's exploitation of the idea of 'travestissement' (in French, 'disguise' as well as the contemporary 'transsexualism') began with her self-canonization and the plethora of dress styles and poses it opened up to her (Wilson 1995: 302).

The persona of Saint Orlan acted as a mobilizing ideal that enabled Orlan to multiply energetically her self-representations across media. It was, however, a multiple rather than a single ideal identity; black-clad as well as white virgins feature in the 'Skaï et Sky and vidéo' exhibition and the painted

Figure 3. 'Imaginary credits no. 15', title of the virtual (unmade) film 'For all miracles, consult our tarifs'. Painted cinema poster, acrylic on canvas, 200cm × 300cm, 1986. Photo by Joël Nicolas.

posters of 'Les 20 ans de pub et de ciné de Sainte Orlan', as well as in other performances and videos, with black and white leatherette (*skaï*) among the fabrics used. Gladys Fabre suggests that the black virgin is a Judeo-Christian figure deliberately counterposed to Orlan's Renaissance and high baroque white Madonnas, perhaps alluding to the Old Testament figure of Lilith, Adam's first wife, who was punished by God for her independence. The black virgin indicates that Orlan's incarnations span the entire history of Christianity and are more than just pastiche of the art of one historical period. In her appearance, the fabrics of her dress, and her poses, which are intent rather than ecstatic, the black virgin is a synthesis of the ancient and modern, a lay figure 'more warlike than religious' (Fabre 1984: 6). She suggests autonomy and the refusal of marriage and maternity. Orlan herself wonders 'if the ludic arguments of this black pistol-holding virgin are not mentally killing the white virgin, perhaps too white for our age', and suggests (rather than affirming) that at the end of the twentieth century the white virgin 'is approaching her own metaphysical death, from which she may be reborn anew, free from the history which weighs on her as heavily as marble' (Orlan, quoted in ibid., p.7). In her contestation of the canonical white virgins and saints of

Renaissance and baroque art, the black virgin is a key figure in Orlan's gallery of images of women.

Fabre's essay for the exhibition catalogue 'Skaï et sky and vidéo' examines the striking dualisms of representation and iconography in Orlan's work up to 1984. For Fabre, the aesthetic which best suited Orlan's purposes in her self-portraiture as a saint is a non-historically specific conception of the baroque, organized around dualisms at all levels. Baroque architecture, for example, can be shown to be built around two centres, a principle Fabre illustrates at work in 'Mise en scène for a saint', the 10m x 10m x 10m chapel constructed by Orlan in Lyons in 1980. A break in a barrier placed diagonally across the inside of the chapel formed a 'hole' denying the spectator access to the sculpture central to the installation, a resin statue whose face, hands and bared breast were produced from moulds of Orlan's own. This breach in the construction constituted one of the centres: the other was indicated on the ceiling by the pointing hand of the statue – a blank space doubled by the projection of a negative film. Whenever the rotating images projected came to a shot of a breast, a laser beam would light up the breast of the sculpted Madonna, a temporary illuminated link indicating other virtual lines of connection. The entire installation was thus organized around two absent centres pointed out to spectators by their physical passage through it, and by the way their gaze was directed to the ceiling. Another dualism which stood out in this construction (one of the largest and most complex Orlan has made) was the bipolar opposition of the real to the artificial – fake marble which looked more real than the real marble used, modern synthetic materials such as polyester resin and leatherette, thirty live doves and 3,800 white plastic flowers.

Bipolar dualisms of material, structure and form are important constituents of the baroque, and Fabre quotes Orlan saying that its dualism ('a double meaning'), rather than polysemy, is what interests her about it. According to Fabre, what defines the baroque aesthetic precisely is the dynamic balance between these opposing elements, a kind of unresolved dialectic she calls a 'boomerang of meanings refusing synthesis' (Fabre 1984: 12). No part of a baroque structure must dominate the others, and a type of unfinished aesthetic unity is brought about by this lack of a focus for the spectator's gaze, which is constantly relayed from one signifier to the next. Orlan's video of 1984 'Light: mise en scène for a grand fiat' was made to be shown on two video monitors in just this way, and the lower section of the piece 'The Metaphors of the Sacred' was composed of two pairs of panels of images from the performance 'Saint Orlan and the Elders' that exactly mirrored each other. There was harmony rather than conflict between the two sets of panels, but no fixity. The notion of the 'double meaning' is also extended by Fabre to

Figure 4. 'Black virgin and video', 1984. Cibachrome on aluminium, 120 × 175
cm. Photo by Jean-Paul Lefert for the ACE3P photo school, Ivry-sur-
Seine.

Orlan's moving performances, which she reads as structured into two antithetical phases 'without a "happy-end" or conclusion' (ibid.: 13). It seems more difficult to apply the idea of the double meaning to Orlan's 1990s work.

Despite Orlan's declared preference for the baroque, and the importance of it to her 1980 ELAC installation brilliantly argued by Fabre, her aim in this and other works was not the pure reproduction of baroque, or any other style. 'Devastatingly post modern and baroque . . . good and bad taste without synthesis . . . pretend and fake pretend . . . winks to the history of art . . . the serious, the funny, the grotesque' reads a caption in the catalogue of the 1985 joint exhibition with Léa Lublin, 'Histoires Saintes de l'Art'. The Saint Orlan performances, videos and installations all blend multilayered pastiche of sacred themes with contemporary multimedia. This is done with great humour; video monitors appear with the wings of angels, and are sometimes used as pedestals – Saint Orlan literally achieves transcendence through technology rather than any conventional spiritual means. Humour and postmodern playfulness with religious subjects were uppermost too in a 'mise-en-scène for 45 putti and a photo' from 1980, in which children dressed as putti crowd round a considerably larger-than-life photographic sculpture of a naked Orlan sticking out her tongue.[7]

Surgical Dressing

Anyone who has seen pictures of Orlan's operation-performances from 'The Reincarnation of Saint Orlan' does not need reminding of the sheer joy in colour, decoration and theatricality displayed in the décors and costumes designed for them. Deliberately upbeat in style to indicate the genuine pleasure (always insisted upon) she takes in performing this difficult and disturbing material, the flavour of the operation-performances is well conveyed in a description of one of the videos of 'Omnipresence', the seventh in the series:

> On a screen behind, Orlan appears wearing a polka-dot dress and a harlequin's hat. She is dancing in an empty operating theatre. Electronic music bubbles in the background. A man enters, muscular and bare-chested, and removes Orlan's dress. She lies down on the operating table. Surgeons, dressed in black, gather round; Orlan keeps her hat on. The bare-chested man dances, the surgeons prance in

---

7. Another instance of deliberate combination of the sacred and the contemporary through their juxtaposition as theme and media was the presentation of a number of the mise-en-scènes such as 'Saint Orlan and the Elders' in multi-screen version, at a festival of new technologies in Toulouse in 1986.

their Issey Miyake robes, and a mime artist translates proceedings into sign language.[8]

A party atmosphere prevails in the operating theatre while Orlan's surgery is going on. Gone is the hushed sobriety we associate with this hi-tech clinical cell; in its place, in addition to the extraordinary costumes worn by Orlan and the medical personnel, a riot of posters and cut-outs of Orlan from her previous works, the bustle of her associates, music and the hum of the communications technology used to record and broadcast the performance. Props such as baskets laden with exotic fruit and the crosses and devil's fork brandished by Orlan from her supine position on the operating table carry the connotations of high art and religious painting into this weirdly hybrid cultural space. Orlan has carefully specified of her 'Reincarnation' project that 'each operation has its style' (Orlan 1996: 89), all of them styles she wants to promote because they have been marginalized by developments in modernist and contemporary art, but common to all the operation-performances is a playful yet vivid and dramatic aesthetic.

Two top designers who have contributed to the costumes and décors of Orlan's surgical performances are the Japanese Issey Miyake and the leading French couturier Paco Rabanne. The lime-green surgeons' robes, masks and drapes and vivid yellow operating table covers Rabanne came up with for 'Omnipresence' lent decadence and intensity to the proceedings, while also forming a perfectly contrasting backdrop to Orlan's half-blue hair and the red blood spilled during the surgery. The shining silver and multicoloured appliqué work that has long characterized Paco Rabanne's evening wear also appeared on the glamorous costumes of the fourth operation-performance on 8 December 1990. The designs of Issey Miyake, light, fanciful and yet classically elegant, have often been viewed and considered as 'works of art' ever since one of his outfits appeared on the front cover of *Artforum* in 1982, making him an obvious choice to supply the robes and hats for Orlan's operation-performances.[9] Orlan may also have wished to associate her work with the democratic sensibility for which Miyake is known, his credo of versatility as a designer coming from firsts like the one achieved by his autumn/winter 1995 collection, which he showed on a group of women in their eighties.[10]

---

8. Andy Beckett, 'Suffering for her Art', *Independent on Sunday*, 14 April 1996, pp. 18–21 (p. 18).

9. Robert Radford, 'Dangerous Liaisons: Art, Fashion and Individualism', *Fashion Theory*, Volume 2 Issue 2 (1998), pp. 151–64 (p. 155).

10. Susannah Frankel, 'Between the pleats', *Guardian* Weekend, 19 July 1997, pp. 14–19.

Style Appeal: New Crossovers of Art and Fashion

It is not only through the costumes worn during her operation-performances that Orlan's work crosses over from the art world to the world of fashion and style. The blurring of boundaries between these two domains has recently begun to stimulate a lot of debate, and in this section I shall consider Orlan as a visual artist whose career has begun to demonstrate many of the complexities typical of the new crossovers between art and fashion.

'The Reincarnation of Saint Orlan' has in fact caught the attention and interest not only of major designers and couturiers, but of international rock music celebrities such as Peter Gabriel and David Bowie, who gave Orlan the death's head that appears like a kind of emblem in some of the photographs of 'Omnipresence' and proclaimed that she is his 'muse'. As well as being involved as a practitioner in the contemporary art scene, Bowie was on the fringes of body art activity in the 1970s, when images of his glamorous androgyny were very comparable to the photographic transgender self-portraiture of artists like Michel Journiac, Urs Lüthi and Luciano Castelli. It is significant, of course, that Bowie and Peter Gabriel are two stars known for having interests that extend well beyond rock music into the spheres of the visual arts and multimedia. An excellent example of the overlap of Orlan's visual art environment with a celebrity's commercial multimedia interests is Orlan's appearance on 'Eve', the second award-winning CD-Rom produced by Gabriel's Real World multimedia company.[11]

The important figures from the fashion world Orlan has worked with, in addition to Issey Miyake and Paco Rabanne, are the photographer Jürgen Teller, and the designers Jeremy Scott and W&LT. The working aesthetics of each of these figures reveal different dimensions of Orlan's 1990s artistic productions particularly well. Teller, for example, is best known for his aesthetic of 'imperfect beauty' – black and white images, ill-fitting forms, and the cultivation of a 'flawed' look – a style obviously in sympathy with Orlan's distorting reshaping of her facial features. Jeremy Scott, the young American designer who arrived in Paris in 1995 after training in New York and catching the attention of Donatella Versace, produced a first collection in October 1996 that included medical imagery – silhouettes made of hospital sheets – and a second in March 1997 called 'Body Modification'. Scott's inspirations – his homages to glamour, use of new synthetic fabrics and a look mixing couture and sportswear he describes as 'luxury avant-garde' –

---

11. *Eve* was completed at the end of 1996 and won five international awards and citations, including the prestigious Milia D'Or, at Cannes in February 1997.

seem particularly close to the styles Orlan has cultivated in the operating theatre.[12]

The clothes of W&LT, an acronym for the Antwerp-based designer Walter Van Beirendonck, have a futuristic dimension that closely matches the technological strain in Orlan's work. W&LT is open about his interest in American body artists Paul McCarthy and Mike Kelley, as well as declaring himself 'very fascinated' by Jeff Koons and Bill Viola, and a fan of everything by the film director David Lynch, a master of the weird and the disturbing. W&LT paid homage to Orlan in one of his *défilés* by making up his models with bumps on their foreheads like those surgically acquired by Orlan in 'Omnipresence' (Orlan 1998b: 67). The aesthetic preferences shown by this idea were very obvious in his Spring-Summer 1998 collection 'A Fetish for Beauty', which included a section called 'Birds from Outer Space'. Bandaged heads, goggles for eyes and mouth and monstrous masks featured among these designs, adding up to an aesthetic of mutilation and monstrosity advertised by the slogans: 'I Scare Myself. Humans are monsters are humans. I'm deranged. Who are today's freaks? Mutilate-radiate-fascinate'. The key characteristics of the great majority of W&LT's clothes are their playfulness, practicality and simple, colourful-yet-futuristic forms, but monsters and science fiction have recently been making regular appearances. Themes of his Summer 1997 collection 'Welcome Little Stranger' included "ET" and "UFO", and during New York fashion week 1999 he displayed his fascination for the dialogue between fashion and the cyberworld by installing ten interactive windows containing tall, shiny antennaed figures at Bloomingdales, the leading New York department store. W&LT's website has links to two CD-Roms that allow the fashion surfer to create his/her own cyber-face, and he sees the internet and the new communications technologies as extremely important for both the design-based and commerical sides of the future of the fashion world.[13]

Orlan's involvement with these major figures from fashion and design is entirely in keeping with the appeal she has begun to have for the style magazine, that can be seen as an area 'where the cultures of art and fashion appear to be most inextricably interfused' (Radford 1998: 153). The mutual cross-fertilization of art and fashion is observable throughout the twentieth

12. Material on Jeremy Scott taken from the websites www.andam.culture.fr/andam/ laureats/scottf.html & www.papermag.com/stylin/parisfall98/jeremy_scott/jeremy_scott.html.

13. Interview with W&LT by Andras W. Viehr for *Medialab*, excerpted on W&LT's website, www.walt.de/, from which all the material in this paragraph is drawn. The site's main colours are pink and fluorescent green, and over the W&LT logo is written 'Kiss the Future!', one of his preferred slogans.

century and particularly strongly at certain moments, such as in the Surrealist movement, but as a phenomenon it has begun to gather pace in the 1980s and 1990s. The critic Sung Bok Kim cites Yves Saint Laurent's 25-year retrospective exhibition at the Costume Institute of the New York Metropolitan Museum of Art in 1983 as the start of the 'controversy' caused by fashion moving into art spaces (Kim 1998: 52). Since 1996 there have been no less than four international exhibitions on the 'art and fashion' theme: *Mode et Art* in Brussels and Montreal in 1996, the *Biennale di Firenze: Il Tempo e La Moda* in Florence in 1996 (also partly shown at New York's Guggenheim museum in 1997), *Assuming Positions*, covering 'new crossovers in Fashion, Art and Pop' at London's ICA in 1997, and *Addressing the Century: 100 Years of Art and Fashion* at London's Hayward Gallery late in 1998 (Radford 1998: 152). The organization of major exhibitions like these could be attributed not to actual new liaisons between artists and couturiers, liaisons which undoubtedly exist, but to an overdue recognition of the vitality of fashion as an aesthetic domain, one that artists draw from and increasingly need to be involved with. Rather than art journals subsuming the discussion of fashion into their pages, as they have traditionally done, fashion writers have begun to put the case for an autonomous aesthetic critical discourse for fashion.[14] A new aesthetic discourse for fashion would quite possibly encourage, rather than discourage, further crossovers and reciprocal influence between the fashion industry and the art world.

As Sung Bok Kim shows, it is not difficult to draw up a list of fashion designers who have worked with visual artists (from Elsa Schiaparelli onwards), or artists who have become directly involved in commercial fashion, such as Keith Haring, Jean Michel Basquiat, and Julian Schnabel (Kim 1998: 55). Orlan's collaborations with Jürgen Teller, Jeremy Scott and W&LT make her a recent addition to the list of internationally recognized artists for whom the boundaries between art and fashion are breaking down. Sung Bok Kim, Robert Radford and the curator of the Hayward Gallery's *Addressing the Century* exhibition all concur that the increasing overlap between the two fields has come about under the influence, since the 1980s, of postmodernism. Kim cites a 1996 article by Roberta Smith, a regular contributor of art criticism to the *New York Times*, in which Smith 'states that the pursuit of fashion's newness is also a basic premise of both modern and postmodern art: "[Fashion] is, in other words, an artworld that [. . .] maintain[s] the myths of newness, breakthroughs, and constant change so basic to both the modernist and postmodernist enterprise" (Smith 1996: 184, quoted in Kim

14. A case powerfully put by Sung Bok Kim in 'Is Fashion Art?' (Kim 1998), and a critical space that the journal *Fashion Theory* has already done much to establish, since 1997.

1998: 56). Kim continues: 'It is very important to note that Smith, as an art critic, explicitly acknowledges that it is no longer true that art, unlike fashion, is eternal and without change' (ibid.). Robert Radford states this point more forcefully:

> Throughout most of the recorded history of art, or rather of commentaries, evaluations and critiques of art, there has existed an almost unquestioned belief that an essential, almost a defining feature of the nature of art is that it should demonstrate the quality of endurance. [. . .] It would seem, however, that all this system of values has recently shifted, now that the conditions of postmodernity and the demonstrations of the New Art History have exposed the insecurity of art's big ideas and have established a widespread cultural permission to recognize the new authenticity of fashion, in the sense that it most accurately reflects and communicates the values and complexities – the anthropological, if not the moral, truths – of contemporary, lived experience. (Radford 1998: 151–2)

Art's 'essential' feature of endurance has been on the wane since the entry of consumer culture into artistic practice in 1960s pop art. A visit to any 1990s exhibition featuring the work of the enormously popular young British artists (Damien Hirst, Sarah Lucas, Jake and Dinos Chapman *et al.*) is enough to convince that although enduring or 'timeless' themes are still being treated, much of the art relies for its effects on speed, humour and visual puns that do not even aspire to outlast their age – without this being a matter of undue concern for the artists.

Amidst highly significant acknowledgements from art critics about art's gradual 'retreat' from the values of endurance, permanence, and transcendence, and the observations by both art and fashion writers of the increasing interpenetration of their respective domains, clear differences can still be identified between art and fashion. Robert Radford's view is that although postmodern culture has transformed the influence of fashion upon art, the exchange is not symmetrical: 'I [. . .] doubt that an equivalent transition has emerged within the recent past out of fashion's relations with art' (Radford 1998: 153). Two of the most obvious differences are the respective relations of the two domains to money – fashion having always been distinguishable from art by its thoroughgoing commercialism – and the issue of individual creativity. In contradistinction to the 'longstanding, genteel tradition – an ideal, at least – that art is the creation of individuals burning bright with lofty inspiration' (Boodro 1990, quoted in Kim 1998: 54), fashion has usually been seen as a thoroughly collective enterprise, dependent on collaboration between designer and producer, and crucially influenced by the models, photographers and writers the couturier employs.

Considering Orlan's recent art practice in the light of these two enduring differences between the fields of art and fashion shows yet again how difficult it is becoming, in contemporary postmodern culture, to arrive at hard-and-fast 'essential' distinctions of quality between different cultural domains. Orlan is not bashful about the financial viability of her artistic projects, and a 1991 article in the French medical journal VST declared that money was a 'major preoccupation' of hers.[15] The expense of the expertise required by the surgical project 'Reincarnation' (in instances where surgeons and other medical personnel have not offered to work for free) has made Orlan's financial undertakings extremely burdensome, and it has simply not been possible for her to remain aloof from some hard commercial decisions about engagements she can and cannot afford to undertake.

The issue of creative individualism in Orlan's work also seems quite a problematic one. Although she is indisputably the main inspiration behind it, and undoubtedly has artistic control of her performances and the exhibition, distribution and sale of her art works, her 1990s practice has become strikingly collective, rather than individual, in the manner of its organization. Apart from the medical and media teams involved in the operations of 'Reincarnation', the production of her exhibited self-images involves the use of ever more sophisticated computer technology – technology she could not personally afford or afford to invest the time to learn to operate. She therefore depends upon the labour of computing specialists. Her life as an artist bears little resemblance to the Romantic myth of individual genius struggling in a garret: it involves constant communication and collaboration with computing personnel, photographers, agents, representatives and the media, as well as the diverse personnel of galleries, museums and other art world establishments.

This collective side to Orlan's artistic practice should not be overestimated, and it does not in any case seriously detract from the forceful individualism that has come across throughout her performance career, as well as in interviews and personal contact with her. What the increasingly collective character of her art practice shows, along with an unconcealed commercialism perhaps more common in the fashion industry than in the world of contemporary art, is that the boundaries between art and fashion have become thoroughly eroded in recent years. As Robert Radford warns, in a type of reminder all too familiar from commentators on the slippery and qualitatively elusive trends of postmodern culture, 'there is a general danger here of

---

15. 'Expertise psychiatrique d'une oeuvre d'art: Orlan', *VST: revue scientifique et culturelle de santé mentale* 23-24, sept–déc 1991, 43–5, p. 44.

category slippage, and there is a need to reach a little beyond the surface appeal of this pairing of art and fashion to clarify, through a set of categorical frameworks, the legitimacy, and even the logical validity, of such an identification of shared territory' (Radford 1998: 153). Orlan is first and foremost a performance and multimedia artist, but the different aspects of her 1990s work I have discussed in this section are an excellent illustration of new and hopefully productive crossovers between art and fashion.

Operations of Redress

In the dress and fashion industries the object is most often the female body. Dress is nothing without a body on which to hang its cut, its folds and its drapes. Other possible uses of the English 'dress' (derived from the Old French *'dresser'* meaning 'to prepare' and/or *'drecier'* meaning 'to arrange'), such as dressing a window, dressing a precious stone or jewellery, remind us of the necessity of having an object to work on. Body and dress function as an opposition which brings more familiar sets of binary oppositions to mind – depth/surface, nature/culture foremost amongst them. If the body, at least prior to the advent of recent feminist theory which has stressed its discursivity and its constructedness, is often thought of as a (natural) object, dress is, by contrast, studied for its signifying properties, and if conceived of as a system, for its semiotics. Dress is social and cultural, even superficial: in the words of the German philosopher and sociologist Georg Simmel, it is the superfluity of adornment which 'allows the mere having of the person to become a visible quality of its being'.[16] The body, on the other hand, contains reaches of depth, privacy and eroticism with which dress cannot compete. Although it might appear possible to see the body as a layered structure, in which skin covers muscles which themselves enclose a patterned intravenous network, it is almost always viewed as a solid, sealed, unflayable entity.

However, a completely different relationship of the body to dress can be imagined – indeed, has been imagined, and is being worn. I would like now to discuss the context which has brought this different relationship about, and consider why the transformation is so important, and how the use of the dressed body in Orlan's work, both pre-surgical and surgical, offers prime illustrations of developments in dress and fashion in the 1980s and 1990s.

16. Georg Simmel, 'Adornment', epigraph to Elizabeth Wilson, *Adorned in Dreams: Fashion and Modernity*, London: Virago Press, 1985.

Piercing, tattooing, scarification and cosmetic surgery make up a group of practices which all involve the skin, and have all risen to prominence in the West in the 1990s. They are a subset of a larger group of activities that includes transsexualism, bodybuilding and rarer practices such as waist training (corsetry has also recently begun to figure prominently in the work of major fashion designers such as Vivienne Westwood) now known by the umbrella term 'body modification'. Many of these practices have emerged into contemporary Western urban culture from very specific removes, social, historical or geographical. For example, tattooing was once the preserve of sailors, gypsies and criminals, while piercing has an intriguing past in aristocratic and royal circles, from whence it somehow found an echo in the punk practice of sticking safety pins through the flesh, as well as through clothing. Chinese footbinding and the rainforest Indians who wear plates in their lips (the Paduong of Burma) are examples of body modification practices in societies remote from Western influence. Those practices that involve the skin all usually imply permanent alteration of the body's appearance, although not all are necessarily carried out with the intention of drawing blood or inflicting pain. Whereas tattooing appears to be a highly individualistic activity, doubtless because of the aspect of designing motifs it implies, scarification seems to be based to a large degree around the shared pleasure of sessions devoted to bloodletting. The rings and studs of piercing are used by some in sexual play, a good indication of the proximity of some of these practices with the culture of sadomasochism.[17]

In all these body modification activities, it is the skin which is being worked on. The skin has become a site of investigation, and an element in the dress of the people whose bodies have been scarred, pierced or tattooed. In the same way in which, as a viewer, it is difficult to ignore a scar or other disfigurement visible on the body of a person passed in the street, the eye is drawn to the scarification patterns, or the point at which the pierce has been inserted, on someone evidently practising body modification. The identificatory sensibility which comes into play when viewing skin altered by an activity such as piercing or scarring, I am suggesting, makes its wearer even more noticeable than someone sporting the latest fashion (or the latest technology) in design or fabrics. At the same time, the advertisement of the skin which accompanies certain kinds of body modification, and the growing currency of skin alteration as a cultural practice amongst Western urban populations, means that it is becoming impossible not to admit it to 'the fashion system'.

---

17. The material summarized in this paragraph is drawn from Linda Grant, 'Written on the Body', *Guardian* Weekend, 1 April 1995, pp. 12–20.

The role of the skin in thinking about the body's place as the object of art, theatre or performance is an issue philosophers and cultural critics have recently begun to address. In a paper entitled 'Rewriting the Skin', Dave Boothroyd focuses on the ethical significance of the skin 'and of being-in-a-skin' in the texts of philosopher Emmanuel Levinas, situating his enquiry as part of the broader subject of 'the nature of ethics in post-humanist times'.[18] To do this, he discusses particularly Levinas's *Otherwise than Being or Beyond Essence*, where 'the skin figures prominently in [Levinas's] account of vulnerability as the "condition" for the ethical relation to the Other' (Boothroyd 1996: 1). Vulnerability and sensibility are key terms in Levinas's investigation of ethics, and the skin is one term around which this investigation is organized.

Boothroyd enumerates three aspects of Levinas's discussion of the skin that he thinks warrant discussion:

> Firstly, there is the fact that the skin is, in every sense, the organ of sensibility: it is not the sense of touch alone that is 'of the skin'. The retina of the eye, the tympan of the ear and the mucous membranes of the nose and mouth are all skin-sites of incarnate sensational intensity. Secondly the skin is, 'without metaphor' – a phrase Levinas is fond of and to which we must return – the boundary between the me and the non-me and gives me the sense of my being an interiority in relation to exteriority. Thirdly, as a theme, or a trope at the very least, the skin can be figured in relation to the logic of the border, its undecidability, and with this comes a whole range of issues related to the limits of philosophy. (ibid.: 1)

As will shortly become apparent, the skin's role as the border of the body is highly relevant to my discussion of dress and the skin, and the skin as dress, in Orlan's work and other body modification practices. What I want to draw from Boothroyd's discussion first and make relevant to my analysis of the skin in Orlan's work is the shift in emphasis Levinas effects, in *Otherwise than Being*, towards a philosophical perspective on the skin, and the implications of this shift for the skin's ethical significance. In *Otherwise than Being* Levinas brings together sensibility and the ethical. Whereas in the earlier *Totality and Infinity* Levinas's discussions of sensibility had supported an account of a separate and individuated 'I', whose sensibility was not involved in the face-to-face relation with the Other and therefore in the ethics Levinas was outlining,[19] in *Otherwise than Being*, sensibility becomes 'the only

---

18. Dave Boothroyd, 'Rewriting the Skin', unpublished? paper given at the 'Sensual Writing' conference, University of Aberdeen, July 1996, henceforth Boothroyd 1996, p. 1.

19. *Otherwise than Being*, p. 118.

possible basis upon which an alterity which does not originate with me, which does not appear in a theme of mine, as another "for-me", can be acknowledged'.[20]

This increased ethical importance Levinas gives to sensibility in *Otherwise than Being* implies a concomitantly greater role for the skin. Boothroyd explains Levinas's conception of sensibility:

> The term 'sensibility' in Levinas names neither the capacity of a subject nor a concept of reflection; it is in-between what empiricist sensualism, on the one hand, considers to be unthought 'pure sensation' and what phenomenology, on the other, regards as the object of consciousness. (ibid.: 5).

Levinas expresses this 'in-between' by saying that 'a thermal, gustative or olfactory sensation is not primarily a *cognition* of pain, a savor, or an odour' (ibid.: 5, my emphasis). Sensation can only become 'an experience of . . ., a consciousness of . . ., [by] placing itself before the being exposed in its theme'.[21] In *Otherwise than Being* Levinas says that his analyses will follow the signifying of sensibility *before* it becomes represented in a theme. He insists, in other words, on reversing the intentionality which allows a sensation to become an object of consciousness.

At the same time, however, he gives greater importance to the skin as the marker of the 'separation' characterizing the 'I'.[22] Although the accounts of sensibility in *Totality and Infinity* and *Otherwise than Being* differ so vitally, there is continuity in the accounts of separation. Maintaining a skin-individuated 'I' alongside an enhanced understanding of sensibility allows the conclusion that in *Otherwise than Being*, it is the skin, as marker of the separation of the sensible subject, which is the condition of the approach of the Other to me. As Boothroyd puts it, 'the superindividuation of the ego [. . .] is the condition for the reversed intentionality which throughout *Otherwise than Being* is held to account for the "obligation", or, my "being-for-the-other". This obligation which depends on *separation at the level of sensibility*, comes to me from beyond myself, unsolicited, undecided by me' (ibid.: 6, my emphasis). In this development of Levinas's ethics, the skin assumes a vital role – not as figure or metaphor, but as literal marker of the individuating boundaries of the incarnate ethical subject. The enhanced

---

20. One place in which this non-relation of sensibility and the ethical is made evident is at the opening of the first section of Section III of *Totality and Infinity*, 'Sensibility and the Face', where Levinas asks how 'the epiphany as a face determine[s] a relationship different from that which characterizes all our sensible experience?' (*Totality and Infinity: An Essay on Exteriority*, trans. by Alphonso Lingis, Martinus Nijhoff, The Hague, 1969, p. 187).

21. *Otherwise than Being*, p. 65, my emphasis.

22. the "superindividuation of the ego [. . .] consists in being in itself, in its skin", ibid.

importance of the skin as an ethical site is an issue I shall return to in later chapters; it is the role of the skin as marker of bodily boundaries which I want to develop further in this chapter, in the final section.

Returning now to the larger issue framing this section, the late twentieth (re-)entry of skin into 'dress code', the particular point I want to make is that accepting the skin as an element of 'dress code' does not just represent an enlargement of what we conventionally understand by 'dress'. It does represent such an enlargement, but it also implies at least two other important changes. The first of these is a change in the status of skin. This takes place through the destabilization of the binary oppositions which the semiotics of dress leaves in place. The skin is the border or limit between the inner body and the outer body (the visible body). It is the container on which the distinction of inside and outside depends. The skin, it begins to become apparent, is central to the underpinning of a metaphysical conception of the body. Whereas the skin has traditionally been conceived of as a 'natural' layer or membrane, it becomes, when body modification practices are admitted as forms of dress, as 'cultural' as jeans or polyester.

The second change, related to but perhaps outstripping the first, is a challenge to the traditional metaphysical definition of the body, in which the skin acts as its container or its 'envelope' (to borrow a figure from Luce Irigaray's reading of phallogocentric philosophy).[23] The involvement of the skin, as the border site between clothes and the body, in the definition of dress, troubles the delimitation of the body as the object which is to be dressed. This challenge to the very concept of the skin as bodily container is one pinpointed by the French psychoanalyst Eugénie Lemoine-Luccioni, whose book *La robe* was partly inspired by Orlan, and which contains a chapter on Orlan's pre-surgical work.[24] As Lemoine-Luccioni puts it, 'Once the skin is removed, there is no body left' (Lemoine-Luccioni 1983: 98). This insight – that the involvement of the skin in cultural practices (and in Orlan's case, in her surgical performances) challenges conventional definitions of dress *and* of the body – would seem to have implications for all art forms and practices – theatre, performance, fashion – which can take the body as their object. Given its most radical interpretation, it completely rewrites the textuality of dress, allowing the body 'itself' to be read as a kind of multilayered outfit of clothing. Printed on the sleeve of one of Orlan's assistants during one operation was the phrase 'The body is but a costume'.

23. 'La différence sexuelle', *Ethique de la différence sexuelle*, Editions de Minuit 1984.

24. Lemoine-Luccioni says of the genesis of her book, in the preface, 'Then Monique Veaute introduced me to Orlan, and I knew from the start where my own enquiry would lead me' (Lemoine-Luccioni 1983: 7).

Returning for a moment to the relationship of the skin to clothing proposed by Lemoine-Luccioni as an alternative to the familiar one, however, we can see that it neatly describes the crossover of the skin and dress that occurs in body modification practices: 'We prefer to consider the garment as equivalent to a second skin, and skin as equivalent to a sort of undergarment' (ibid.). An inversion or invagination of this type is exactly what Orlan demonstrated in a performance in Lisbon in 1981, when she ran through crowded streets in an opaque black 'chasuble' bearing a life-sized photographed print of her naked body. A policeman directing traffic who wanted to arrest her was persuaded by Orlan that there was nothing illegal about wearing such eye-catchingly printed clothing; it is, on the contrary, a mark of high fashion. The designer who has recently commercialized the printing of photographs onto separates in this way is none other than Issey Miyake, who created the costumes for Orlan's 1993 operation-performance 'Omnipresence' (in 1996 I saw a presenter on French television's cult Canal Plus programme 'Nulle part ailleurs' wearing a dress made by Miyake with a life-sized nude torso printed on it). A further performance of Orlan's illustrating an invagination of the body and dress is described by Tanya Augsburg:

> During one performance at the Louvre, as part of a collective performance organized by Jean Dupuy on 16 October 1978, Orlan revealed her dress underneath her black coat and skirt only to rip open the geometric pubic triangle, displaying her pubic hair underneath. Once revealed, Orlan pulled out her preshorn and reglued pubic hair to uncover her shaved genital area. With an already dipped paintbrush, Orlan covered up her nakedness, first, by painting her pubis black, and then by holding a white artist's palette before her "painting" as if it were a fig leaf. (Orlan 1980: 202–3; Augsburg 1998: 295)[25]

Despite mentioning the trope of invagination so strikingly illustrated by Orlan's Lisbon and Louvre performances in her redefinition of the relationship of dress and the skin, Lemoine-Luccioni does not use it to advance questioning about the way it troubles the definition of the body. She does refer to the

---

25. A lot more than just a crossover of the body and dress is clearly going on in this performance, and Augsburg continues: 'Highlighting her self-conscious appropriation of the romantic and modernist conceptions of the virile male artist who uses his paintbrush as a metaphorical penis, Orlan next inserted her paintbrush through the hole of the palette to display the profile of her "erect" paintbrush. With this extremely condensed performance, Orlan seems to be acting out what Lynda Nead interprets as the structure of penis-as-paintbrush metaphor: "the canvas is the empty but receptive surface; empty of meaning – naked – until it is inscribed and given meaning by the artist"' (Nead 1992: 56; Augsburg 1998: 295).

work of fellow-psychoanalyst Didier Anzieu, whose concept of the 'Moi-peau' ('I-skin' or 'ego-skin'), posits a coincidence of the child's developing ego with a 'narcissistic envelope':

> I employ the term I-skin to refer to a figuration used by the child's ego during the early stages of its development to represent itself as an ego containing psychic contents, on the basis of its experience of the body's surface.[26]

Anzieu's concept of the 'Moi-peau' radicalizes the importance of the projection of bodily surfaces to the formation of the ego seen in Freud's 'bodily ego' and in Lacan's concept of the imaginary. As with Emmanuel Levinas's work on the skin, the incorporation of the skin as organ of sensibility into ego-formation suggests the ego is a more sensitive and more fragile entity than it is often considered to be. But for Anzieu the skin appears to function as a bodily container whose boundaries are not put into question; the concept 'Moi-peau' implies a coincidence of the limits of the body and the limits of the ego.

Lemoine-Luccioni does, however, comment on the implication of the skin in questions of being: 'Skin is disappointing [. . .] But it does nonetheless suggest something to do with being' (Lemoine-Luccioni 1983: 95). In a formulation of which part is cited by Orlan at the beginning of all her performances, she continues:

> It is quite clear that the only possession he has ("my skin is all I have to my name" is a common expression) weighs heavily on him. It is still in excess, because having and being do not coincide, and because having is a cause of misunderstanding in all human relationships: I have the skin of an angel but I am a jackal, the skin of a crocodile, but I am a dog; a black skin but I am white; the skin of a woman but I am a man. I never have the skin of what I am. There is no exception to the rule because I am never what I have. (ibid.)

The skin pinpoints the disjuncture between having and being which occurs in Georg Simmel's reflections on adornment. If skin did not figure in analyses of dress during the stage of modernity commented on by Simmel, it does in the 1990s.

In the final chapter of *La robe* devoted to Orlan, Lemoine-Luccioni returns to the question of the closure of the body, stating 'The body is not closed. Nor is the garment which envelops it' (ibid.: 137). Orlan's interest is not in weaving (that most archetypally feminine of activities) and the texturing of surfaces; she is more concerned with the opposite operations of rupturing

---

26. Didier Anzieu, *Le Moi-peau*, Dunod 1995 (Bordas 1985 pour la première édition), p. 61.

and opening apparently hermetic wrappings and coverings: 'Orlan un-weaves; she lacerates every enveloping layer' (ibid.: 143). This is most dramatically applied to the skin in Orlan's surgical work, but has also featured in her 'living sculptures'. In the first part of the Saint Theresa action of which different 'tableaux' were photographed for use in subsequent artworks, Orlan's breast emerged to be brandished from within the ornate drapery of her robes. (The second part of the action was more overtly destructive, including the cutting of the 'drapé' into rags.)[27] Amidst echoes of theatrical statues magically coming to life Orlan at a stroke pinpoints the specificity of performance and rebels against the passivity and chastity of an objectified subject of classical art history. The actions of opening and cutting she performs here with costume have been developed and radicalized in her surgical project. In the exhibition of photographic plates of her surgeries which toured the UK in 1996/7, a barely suppressed jubilation could be felt in the words accompanying the enlarged photo-plate of Orlan's face being cut away from the side of her head, 'The body is open . . .'

Woman in Space: Variations on Containment

In the final section of this chapter I would like to return to the notion of the body as container, and consider it more closely, by discussing a series of Orlan's performances which preceded 'The Reincarnation of Saint Orlan'. Dress again figures centrally in these performances, which are the 'mesurages' or measurings first executed by Orlan in 1976 in Nice, and subsequently in 1977 at the Centre Georges Pompidou, in 1978 in Strasbourg, and in 1979 in Lyon, at a festival of performance art organized by Orlan and Hubert Besacier. Further measurings took place at the Guggenheim Museum in New York in 1983, and again at the Centre Georges Pompidou in 1984 (Wilson 1996: 11–12).

What Orlan is doing when she places her body into a specific environment as a measure can be seen as an instance or citation of anthropometry, which is a science consisting of the collection of the measurements of different human

---

27. 'The most important performances: *The Draping, The Baroque,* were done dressed up in my trousseau as a madonna (Centre Georges Pompidou, Paris: Halles de Skarbek, Brussels: Pinacothèque, Ravenna; Bologna Theatre; Arc Biennale, Paris). These slow-motion performances were constructed as an enfolding and unfurling. At the end, I unswaddled a bundle resembling a little child made of a forty metres ribbon of the same fabric. Inside was a painted bread sculpture with a blue crust and red crumb, which I ate in public often to the point of vomiting' (Orlan 1996: 84).

bodies for use by professional engineers and designers. According to Anne Balsamo, a feminist commentator on technology and the gendered body, anthropometry is a field with which many cosmetic surgeons have some familiarity, because of its interest in the establishment of ideals and norms of measurement which can then be used for the purposes of design. Balsamo explains:

> Of course it makes a great deal of sense that measurement standards and scales of human proportions are a necessary resource for the design of products for human use; in order to achieve a "fit" with the range of products from office chairs to office buildings, designers must have access to a reliable and standardized set of body measurements. (Balsamo 1996: 59).

The parallel of Orlan's measurings with the practice of anthropometry brings out two aspects of her actions. The first is that her body is female, and that its use as a measure is already different from the use of the male body that has traditionally lain behind the construction of systems of measurement. Some measures, such as the foot (and other less common ones such as the cubit, which is equivalent to the length of the forearm) are so familiar that we tend to forget they are based on the male and not the female body. Orlan's use of her woman's body as a measure cannot contribute to the imagining of universals which take the male body as a norm. Instead, her actions suggest that she envisages a different, female universal – perhaps that there should be, effectively, a double universal, as in the thinking of Luce Irigaray.[28] Orlan's measurings should perhaps be described as the practice of gynometry rather than anthropometry, a substitution of femaleness for maleness which highlights the gendered nature of a subject of (practical) science too often and for too long assumed to be 'neutral', or free of the fundamental bodily modifiers of gender and race.

There is a striking affinity between Orlan's measurings and the reflections on the relationship of gender to the use of the body in space made by Christine Battersby, in her article 'Her Body/Her Boundaries' (Battersby 1993). Within this larger problematic, the specific issues Battersby investigates are containment and bodily boundaries, and she mentions fashion and cosmetic surgery as highly significant methods by which women may discipline the boundaries of their bodies (Battersby 1993: 33). Battersby's focus, however, is the idea of the body as a container for the inner self, an idea which she finds radically foreign to her own (female) experience of what it is to inhabit a body. Seeking an alternative to the view that envisages the body as 'a container in which

28. See particularly *J'aime a toi*, Editions Grasset & Fasquelle, 1992.

Figure 5. 'Measuring' performance in the Piazza S. Pietro of the Vatican, Rome, 1974. Photo by Jean-Luc Waumann.

the self is inside and protected from the other by boundaries which protect against and resist external forces, whilst also holding back internal forces from expansion', Battersby turns not to a poststructuralist deconstruction of borders, but to 'a metaphysics revisited from the perspective of gender – in order to reconstitute the inside/outside, self/other, body/mind divides [. . .] The move into feminist metaphysics opens up other possibilities which allow us to theorise a 'real' beyond the universals of an imagination or a language which takes the male body and mind as ideal and/or norm' (ibid.: 32).

One alternative Battersby suggests to the experience of the female body as container – which she maintains may not be a typically female experience – is that 'I [speaking as a woman] construct a containing space around me, precisely because my body itself is not constructed as the container' (ibid.: 34). The choice of enclosing architecture as the environment of Orlan's measurings indicates that what is going on is very akin to this construction of an extra-bodily container. Whilst the performance of the action of measuring in art galleries and other art spaces may be seen as a relatively straightforward claim upon those spaces by a woman artist, the choice of an ecclesiastical edifice for a measuring, in the case of the Musée St-Pierre in Lyon, a former monastery, can be read both as an assertion of the identity of Saint Orlan and as the appropriation of a space heavily imbued with the history and imagery of the established patriarchal Church.

Battersby ends 'Her Body/Her Boundaries' by specifying that the new feminist metaphysics she is calling for 'will not appeal to an unsymbolised imaginary' (ibid.: 38). This introduces the final idea I would like to focus on here, which is the idea of the female imaginary, in relation both to Orlan's work with dress and use of her body in space.

Twentieth-century philosophy offers a number of different theorizations of the imaginary. An extremely lucid summary and comparison of these is given by Margaret Whitford in the third chapter of her study of Luce Irigaray (Whitford 1991). According to Whitford, one major source for the notion of the imaginary is phenomenology ('according to Sartre's definition, the imaginary is the intentional object of the imagining consciousness' (ibid.: 54)), and another the work of the French philosopher Gaston Bachelard, for whom the imaginary is also a function of the imagination. Perhaps the dominant theorization of the imaginary in recent years, however, has been the Lacanian one. Lacan's concept of the imaginary is related to his highly influential concept of the mirror stage, according to which a child's first glimpse of a unified image of its body is a key moment in the formation of its identity. Whereas the mirror stage describes a particular moment in childhood development, the imaginary designates an entire order which overlaps with the pre-Oedipal mirror stage, but also describes subsequent operations of the ego, such as identification and falling in love. Although the imaginary is a concept particular to Lacan, and not formulated as such by Freud, the role of the body-image in its formation has striking similarities with Freud's notion that the mental projection of bodily surfaces contributes significantly to the formation of the ego.

One idea which follows from the psychoanalytic conception of the imaginary in particular, is that it (the imaginary) revolves around the role of the specular image in mental life. Since this image is based upon the outline or 'envelope' of the body, dress, as well as body shape, will play a vital part in imaginary formations. Furthermore, the work of psychoanalysts has revealed that the limits of the body as perceived by the subject can undergo displacement, so that spaces to which the subject feels connected, such as its home, or a particular room in that home, act as extensions of its body image, and are as actively involved in the imaginary as the (dressed or undressed) profile of the body. This imaginary interplay of specular self-image, dress, and inhabited space, noted by Eugénie Lemoine-Luccioni at several points in *La robe*,[29] indicates a way of associating them different from those mentioned hitherto, and one which is highly suggestive where Orlan's work with all three 'envelopes' is concerned.

The theorist of the imaginary Whitford herself is interested in is, of course, Luce Irigaray. Whitford explains Irigaray's imaginary as follows:

[Irigaray] conflates in a single term the phenomenological definition of the imaginary (the conscious, imagining and imaging mind) with the psychoanalytic definition (the unconscious, phantasying mind) and can move fluidly between one and the other. (ibid.: 54)

Another thinker of the imaginary with whom Irigaray has much in common is Cornelius Castoriadis, who, in addition to formulating a critique of Lacan's definition of the term, 'deploys the concept of the imaginary in an explicit attempt to understand the persistence of social formations and the possibility of changing them'. (ibid.: 60). Like Irigaray, Castoriadis employs the term 'imaginary' to describe both a primary creative force in the mind (conscious or unconscious), and a social formation. However, the last important feature of Irigaray's imaginary distinguishes her from Castoriadis too. This is that for Irigaray, the imaginary is sexuate [*sexué*]; in other words, it becomes meaningful to speak of a male and a female imaginary respectively, because the imaginary bears the morphological marks of the gendered body. The body which shapes the social imaginary is not an empirical but already a symbolic one, in which a metaphorical relationship to anatomy lends particular shape-related values to thought and to culture. This enables Irigaray to argue that Western patriarchal culture is and always has been shaped by the male imaginary, meaning that its cultural products carry the characteristics of male morphology – unity, linearity and closure. The traditional dominance of the male imaginary means that the female imaginary has been suppressed and not thoroughly theorized. Several definitions of it remain possible, however, all of which are characterized by fragmentation, fluidity, and openness (and there are important similarities here between Irigaray and the 'new topologies' cited by Battersby as important to her new metaphysics of

29. 'At the moment when specular experience began, when his image appeared in the mirror under the active guarantee of the mother's look, he gave himself a frame. This specular image, which in Lacanian algebra is written i (o), is man's first garment' (Lemoine-Luccioni 1983: 78). Further references are p. 82, p. 90 (in the chapter 'Specular image – clothing – house' ('Image spéculaire – vêtement – maison'), p. 111).

boundaries, whose basic paradigms would be those of potentialities, flow and permeability). Whitford is careful to point out that these descriptions of the female imaginary should not be read in an essentialist manner, but 'as a description of the female as she appears in, and is symbolized by, the western cultural imaginary' (ibid.: 56).

Returning to Battersby's wish to avoid appealing to an unsymbolized imaginary, the process of undergoing analysis, in which diverse psychic material not previously dealt with by the subject is expressed in language or represented (symbolized) in some other way, can be described as a process of symbolization. However, if the imaginary is considered as a social concept, the issue of the unsymbolized imaginary has more far-reaching ramifications. It suggests that the feminine as a category is consigned to unmodifiable 'dereliction' within the symbolic order, unless it can be re-symbolized within that order, a transformation of the conditions of representation as they relate to sexual difference.

I would like to suggest that in Orlan's work, both approaches to the imaginary are relevant, but that the latter is much more pertinent to those of her actions which revolve principally around dress and the use of her body in space. In other words, I do not want to exclude the consideration of Orlan as a psychoanalytic 'case', whose singular relationship to the symbolic order may be being seen (and may even be being worked through) in her performance projects. This is an approach to her work which has already been taken and which yields fascinating observations.[30] But despite the interest of this deployment of the imaginary/symbolic relationship, the Irigarayan insistence on the gendered and social character of the imaginary, and its potential for social and political transformation, seems to me to offer a much readier reading of actions such as Orlan's public measurings. This is simply because the representations of which these actions consist are (always) already thoroughly public, thoroughly social. In the instance of Orlan's use of her body as a measure, the emphasis may be seen to be upon the visibility of a solitary woman's body in a public space, a representation which emphasizes her femaleness, and implicitly comments upon the gender-bias both of systems of measurement and of the differing relationships of the two sexes to geometry, architecture, design, and space.

A further aspect of Orlan's measurings has even more striking resonances with the definitions of the female imaginary offered by Irigaray. This is the ritual washing of the clothes worn by Orlan during the performance, which

---

30. 'Expertise psychiatrique d'une oeuvre d'art: Orlan', *VST: revue scientifique et culturelle de santé mentale* 23–24, sept–déc 1991, 43–5.

also takes place in public. The dirty water left over from this washing is then placed in sealed jars as 'relics' of Saint Orlan, a procedure also used with flesh extracted from Orlan's body by liposuction in 'Reincarnation':

> The 'maculae', stains, the sweat and dust-infused water [. . .] was collected in a bowl and then transferred to containers sealed with wax as relics. The Virgin, conceived 'immaculately', without stain, counters the tradition of the bride's display of bloodied linen after the wedding night [. . .]. [Orlan's] 'measuring' performances provoked violently sexual reactions: she was spat upon, insulted as 'a woman of the streets'; the trial of measurement passes through filth. (Wilson 1996: 11–12)

In this way residual traces of the contact of Orlan's clothing with her body and with the environment are preserved, traces which could be seen as emblematic of the 'scraps' and 'debris' characteristic of an emergent, alternative female imaginary, as sketched out by Irigaray (Whitford 1991: 59, 67). Another account of the measuring which took place at the Musée St-Pierre in Lyon in 1979 reveals that chalk-markings made by Orlan of each repositioning of her body in the measuring constitute another trace of the unfamiliar passage of a female body through a space whose architecture and form (a quadrangle of cloisters) connotes predominantly the closure and unity of patriarchal representation.[31] The account also describes the vigour with which Orlan carries out the washing of her clothes, described as 'an act of pressure', and the quasi-jubilation which she shows after exerting this effort. This energy put by Orlan into the act of preserving representations of the contact of her body with the environment is suggestive of the kind of 'excess' Irigaray also associates with a female imaginary which 'jams the machinery' of patriarchal representation and can be seen seeking alternative forms, or alternatives to the the traditional conception of 'form' itself.

An unquestioned assumption of much work in performance is that the body constitutes the 'theatrical' object par excellence. One aim of this study of Orlan is to investigate the possibility that she is undoing the very notion of the body as aesthetic object usually taken as the basis of performance and theatre. A number of other performance artists, such as Stelarc and Marina Abramovic, have done or are currently doing work focusing on the skin, and on the question of whether the body can or should be thought of as a container; by focusing on dress, the skin and the definition of the body, Orlan's artistic practice constantly raises and dramatizes similar issues. As I have suggested by drawing on the ideas of Irigaray and Christine Battersby, a

---

31. *Premier Symposium International d'Art Performance de Lyon*, Editions du Cirque Divers, 1980.

Figure 6. Street measuring, 1978; final pose of action by the Orlan-body, holding up relic of dirty water from dress washed in public. Black and white photo, 110cm × 165cm.

reformulation of the problem of bodily boundaries and the body in space is most usefully approached via a parallel discussion of gender difference. Irigaray's concept of the female imaginary claims dynamic and transformative potential for symbolic practice involving the female body. A reminder of some words of Orlan's about her work as a woman artist is timely at this point: 'Art can, art must change the world, it's its only justification' (Orlan 1996: 85).

Hard (core) Images: Orlan's Carnal Art, the Monstrous-Feminine, and Spectatorship

How Do I Look?

The acclaimed transsexual and cultural theorist Sandy Stone makes the following comment on the relationship between performer and audience established by Orlan's surgical project 'The Reincarnation of Saint Orlan': 'It's a fine edge to walk between holding one's audience in thrall, or sending them rushing for the exits, or making them puke on their shoes. The trick is to hold them in thrall and *still* have them puking on their shoes. Orlan approaches this ideal more closely than any performer I have known' (Stone 1996: 43). For Stone, entranced revulsion is an effect contemporary performance should be aiming at – a response elicited by the explicit body art of Californian Ron Athey, who is HIV positive and uses blood in his performances, or visual artist Andres Serrano, whose images defy taboos in order to investigate them. In Orlan's performances, and in the public presentations of her work that include screenings of the films of her operations, responses have obviously varied from venue to venue, depending on location, and on the composition of the audience. The commonest audience reaction, however, has been a mixture of fascination and disgust that sometimes includes an aggressive element. Jim McClellan recounts an incident at Orlan's 1994 appearance at London's ICA, when a woman from the audience stood up to announce 'You're just the sickest person I've ever met,' and concluded her intervention with the words 'It makes me want to give you a good slap' (McClellan 1994: 38–40).

In this chapter I shall explore the reception and viewing of Orlan's work. Drawing particularly on her cosmetic surgery project, but also on important earlier performances such as *Documentary Study. The Head of Medusa*, I shall work towards an interpretation of the type of viewing Orlan's artistic practice entails. What kind of spectator is drawn to her performances, installations and multimedia artworks, and what relationship is set up between spectator and performer when s/he views them? I shall start with a brief review of the reception of 'The Reincarnation of Saint Orlan', since it is the project which has brought Orlan international renown, and has been most commented upon outside the journals and specialized publications of the art press and the academy. The second section of the chapter will look at 'carnal art' in more detail, and will consider the 'blasphemy' Orlan claims is central to it. The third, longest part of the chapter will explore in depth the questions of spectatorship already introduced. Employing the ideas of feminist film critics Carol Clover and Barbara Creed, it will first address the general questions raised by looking at Orlan's work outlined above. It will then turn to the particular area of the spectatorship of feminine monstrosity that has recently been explored in psychoanalytically-inspired feminist writing on film, and explore the relevance of these theories to Orlan's performances of the 'monstrous feminine', from the 1970s onwards.

'The Reincarnation of Saint Orlan' has been received in a remarkably broad range of venues, from the world's biggest galleries of contemporary art to local arts centres, and from academic conferences to television studios, where Orlan has appeared alongside celebrities such as Madonna. (Madonna was allegedly keen to associate her own minor surgical operations with Orlan's 'at least until Orlan gave her a little bottle containing a piece of her thigh at the end of the show'.[1]) In a parallel manner, the critical reception of the project has been formed across an amazing variety of publications, from the monthly international art journals to *People* magazine, on the one hand, and Britain's *The Big Issue* on the other.[2] While serious and sympathetic consideration of Orlan's decision to incorporate cosmetic surgery into her art practice has been forthcoming from many of these publications, the project has also met with an enormous amount of misunderstanding and hostility.

The commonest misinterpretation of the objectives of 'Reincarnation' is the view that Orlan's aim in undergoing surgery is, quite simply, to become more beautiful. According to this reading, Orlan is uncritically imitating the beauty of the icons whose facial features have been digitally combined with her own, and is therefore demonstrating a similar relationship to cosmetic surgery to the majority of ordinary women who elect to undergo it. She is not necessarily just another 'scalpel slave', but her work is recuperable within the ideology of ideal female beauty that governs the practice of cosmetic surgery in the West (and increasingly, worldwide). The type of publication

1. Andy Beckett, 'Suffering for her Art', *Independent on Sunday*, 14 April 1996, pp. 18–21 (p. 18).

2. *The Big Issue* is a weekly magazine written, produced and sold by the homeless in Britain. Orlan gave an interview to Lena Corner for issue no. 177 (15–21 April 1996), p. 10.

where this interpretation has prevailed is the short newspaper article or book review,[3] where a brief mention of Orlan, or the inclusion of a picture of her, suggests that her surgical work is simply a dressy display of a medical practice much in vogue. This tenacity of this type of interpretation is encapsulated by an anecdote Orlan recounts about an occasion organized for her at the *Palace* in Paris after the 1993 trip to New York for 'Omnipresence', the seventh operation-performance, in which she acquired the implants above her eyebrows. The very point of this press conference, attended by about sixty journalists, was to put a stop to misinterpretations by the mainstream media of the objectives of 'Reincarnation':

> I said: "Can you see my face? So you'll stop writing that I want to be the most beautiful woman, that I want the Mona Lisa's forehead or that I want to look like Botticelli's Venus, which is a beauty standard that I'm fighting against". And so, in the next few days, 50% of the articles led with titles like "She wants to be ideal beauty", "She wants Psyché's nose"[. . .] So, I have to conclude not only that I show images that make us blind, but that I also speak words which make us deaf (in the operating room I was always accompanied by a sign language specialist for the deaf and hard of hearing!). (Orlan 1998: 97)

Since this event Orlan has had a policy that any exhibition of images of her work must be accompanied, at some point in its run, by a lecture or presentation given by her in person – an indication that the battle to get the artistic and critical dimension of 'Reincarnation' across to her audience has not been conclusively won. Although the project has unquestionably been taken seriously, and had its critical aims understood, by the international art press and the academy, she cannot count on the same sympathetic reception from the popular press or television.

Misinterpretations lead to hostility, and Orlan has been called a publicity freak and a surgery junkie, and had her mental equilibrium repeatedly called into question. It seems to me that detractors and sceptics share fundamental misplaced assumptions about the directions and objectives of 'Reincarnation'. They assume, first, that only Orlan's external appearance is at issue. History will be able to interpret and pass judgment on Orlan's body modification once she has attained the ultimate image designed at the outset of the project. Her surgical work is assumed to be concerned only with surface and with the visual identity presented by modified features. Interpretations of Orlan's 'horns' – the 'Mona Lisa' implants inserted in her forehead during 'Omnipresence' – are a good illustration of this appearance-driven interpretation.

3. Sarah Dunant, 'Bodies of Opinion', review of Elizabeth Haiken, *Venus Envy* (Johns Hopkins University Press: 1997), *Guardian*, 4 December 1997.

Although the pronounced bumps above her eyebrows may resemble diabolic horns of the kind seen in medieval and Renaissance sacred painting, this reading is not only partial and univocal (ignoring the intended reference in favour of a negative and misogynistic one), it presumes upon Orlan's desire to resemble the horned devils of the painting of whatever period. The aims of 'Reincarnation' are understood to be essentially mimetic. Orlan's own interventions in the interpretations of her project have repeatedly countered this framework of analysis with insistences that straightforward mimetic desire – the desire to resemble (another image) – does not concern her (Orlan 1995). Although her status as an artist of representation required the choice of visual images for her digital self-redesign, she selected the features of Mona Lisa, Venus, Diana, Europa and Psyche not for their appearance, but because of the mythical qualities and attributes these women possessed – the Mona Lisa for the androgyny resulting from the palimpsest of Leonardo da Vinci's self-portrait beneath her image, Venus because of her connection to fertility and creativity, Diana for her insubordination to men and aggressivity as the goddess of hunting, Europa because Gustave Moreau's painting of her is unfinished, and because her look to another continent showed her interest in an unknown future, and Psyche because of her need for love and spiritual beauty (Orlan 1996: 88-9; Rose 1993: 84).

Combining features from a number of art historical icons was a strategy Orlan adopted in order to work against notions of aesthetic unity and identical resemblance (one of the few parallels postwar contemporary art can offer is Andy Warhol's celebrity collages). Her own explanations of her surgical performances, as well as a proportion of the commentary about them, emphasize that 'Reincarnation' was never planned as a quest or pursuit of a single image, beautiful, diabolic or anything in between. The alternative title of the project, 'Image-New Images', 'makes passing reference to Hindu gods and goddesses who change appearances to carry out new deeds and exploits – for me it is about shifting referents, passing from Judaeo-Christian religious iconography to Greek mythology – something that I do after all my operations' (Orlan 1996: 85). Orlan's guiding ideas were plurality and the continuous production of images. What matters most in the project is the *process* of modification. Orlan's manifesto of 'carnal art' (*art charnel*) states that this type of art 'is not interested in its final, plastic result but in the surgical operation-performance and in the modified body as a site of public debate' (Orlan 1997: 2). What it aims at is not a sequence of fixed identities, but a material exploration of the transitional space between them. Orlan's conception and programme of carnal art revolves around certain key ideas about identity, figuration, the body, and the flesh, and in the next section, I shall consider these more closely.

From *'Art Corporel'* to *'Art Charnel'*

Orlan gives 'carnal art' this name in order to distinguish it from the body art (*art corporel*) movement of the late 1960s and 1970s. She acknowledges carnal art's links to precursor body artists such as Gina Pane, Vito Acconci and Bruce Nauman, but insists on its specificity. Carnal art is against a prioris and diktats; it is anti-formalist, anti-conformist, and feminist. It is highly relevant to the ethical questions about the status of the body preoccupying contemporary medicine and biology, and is as much an issue for society and the media as for the art world and artists. Its characteristic styles and genres include parody, the baroque, and the grotesque, elements of which have featured in the design, décor and costumes for each of Orlan's operation-performances. Essentially, though, carnal art is non-programmatic in intent, envisaged as a space in which styles rejected by mainstream art practice can be represented and explored.

An important way in which carnal art differs from earlier body art practice is the recuperation and use of the flesh. In conventional surgery tissue extracted from the patient's body is deemed to be the property of the medical

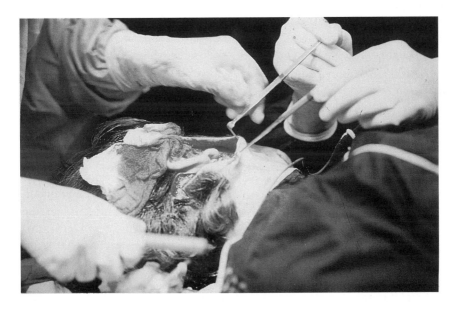

Figure 7. Close-up in red, blue and green on the opening of the body during the 7th operation-performance 'Omnipresence', New York, 21 November 1993. Cibachrome in diasec vacuum, 165cm × 110cm. Photo by Vladimir Sichov for SIPA Press.

profession or the hospital, but Orlan's flesh is appropriatively removed by her from the operating theatre. The use of bodily fluids is no longer a novelty in postwar art, urine having been used in Andy Warhol's oxidation pictures, and recently to more notable effect by Andres Serrano in *Piss Christ* (1987) and Helen Chadwick in *Piss Flowers* (1994). Excrement and urine were both employed by Gilbert and George in their recent set of *Fundamental Pictures*. It is more difficult, though, to list artists whose flesh has been extracted to become the material of the artwork. Orlan's flesh is measured out into a precise number of grammes, encased in resin and framed, then mounted with phrases of text describing carnal art, to form the reliquaries that are sold or go on display in galleries. Her body is a factory, her flesh its product. The object-based work of Orlan's which best illustrates this process is the sequence of large reliquary tablets 'my flesh, the texts and the languages', each of which has at its centre resin-preserved flesh mounted amidst large-printed text of the same passage from Michel Serres' *Le Tiers-Instruit* which Orlan reads during operations, translated into many and little-known languages. Orlan's stated aim for this work is that the translation should continue until all known and dying languages have been exhausted, suggesting that the productivity of her body is being measured against the capacity of language(s) to describe and represent it.

Another work that has made direct use of the body products of Orlan's operations is her drawings in blood. A 'finger drawing in blood' from 1993 is a roughly drawn head whose outline resembles the bandages of a patient of cosmetic surgery – a kind of abstracted, non-resembling self-portrait whose gaping mouth and hollow eyes evoke a ghoulish death's head and/or the anonymous bodily interior opened up to view in Orlan's operations. The artist's blood is not a new substance in body art either, having figured memorably in the work of Gina Pane in the early 1970s, and in the more contemporary performances of Ron Athey. Recently, the use of the performer's blood as artistic material ('blood painting') has been taken up and developed particularly by the Italian-born artist Franko B, who pours his own blood (drawn off beforehand) over his naked, chalked body and surrounding whitened floor space, and goes on to make improvised drawings with it. The strain that bleeding himself puts upon his body means that Franko B limits his 'blood performances' to four a year.[4] Other elements of Franko B's acts, such as choreographed slapping sessions, suggest that he, rather than any contemporary female performer, is the direct inheritor of Gina Pane's masochism.

4. *The South Bank Show* on body art, London Weekend Television, 5 April 1998.

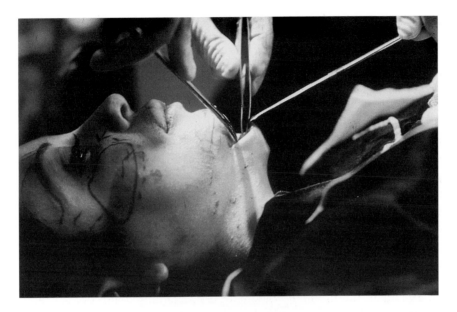

Figure 8. 'The second mouth', 7th operation-performance 'Omnipresence', New
York, 21 November 1993. Cibachrome in diasec vacuum, 165cm ×
110cm. Photo by Vladimir Sichov for SIPA Press.

One way to situate Orlan's intimate exploration of her own flesh, employing psychoanalytic concepts as I shall do in a more sustained fashion in the
third part of this chapter, is as between narcissism and auto-eroticism. Auto-
surgery implies a readiness if not necessarily an active desire to engage with
the carnal materiality of one's own flesh, and so indicates an eroticized
relationship with one's own body. (To see Orlan's surgical project as the
straightforward exhibition of auto-erotic practice, a view invalidated in any
case by the involvement of a surgical team and other performers, would be
to exaggerate this dimension of 'Reincarnation'.) The narcissistic aspect of
carnal art requires more patient tracing, and one which bears in mind Freud's
definition of narcissism as 'ego-libido', that component of the libido that
attaches to the subject's ego but becomes mobile and employed in relationships
with others in psychically important activities such as identification, fantasy
and falling in love. In remarks from Orlan's carnal art manifesto, she confirms
the relevance of narcissism to the project:

carnal art opens 'a new Narcissistic space which is not lost in its own reflection . . .'
So I can see my own body open and without suffering! . . . look again, I can see
myself down to my entrails . . . a new mirror stage! it is in this look into the depths
of my old body that our contemporanaity (sic) is legible . . . (a work of reversibility).

Figure 9. 3 relics 'this is my body this is my software', 'I gave my body to art', 'happening in the operating theatre', soldered metal and burglarproof glass, 10g of my flesh encased in resin, 30cm × 30cm × 5cm, 1993.

While not disputing that carnal art works in a narcissistic space (artists who practice it are self-involved – although as in Freud's deployment of the concept of narcissism, this description does not have morally pejorative overtones), Orlan here takes issue with the Lacanian notion of the mirror stage to which Freud's writings on narcissism pointed the way. The ramifications of this concept in Lacanian theory are many, but most important here is probably the emphasis Lacan's concept places upon the idea of a complete, whole external body image perceived by the child – this wholeness is illusory, but persuades the infant for the first time that its body is unified and coordinated. The child's pleasure in perceiving its body as a clean, smooth, unpunctured entity is a momentous event in the process of ego-formation; what occurs –

Figure 10. Finger drawing in blood, done during the eighth surgical intervention, 1993. 100cm × 70cm.

or begins to occur – in the *stade du miroir* is the conception of what Francette Pacteau, commenting on Freud's essay 'Character and Anal Erotism', refers to as 'an imaginary body, a 'skin-ego' whose unity is premised upon the disavowal of the heterogeneous mass of internal organs, fluids and faeces which lie beneath its surface' (Pacteau 1994: 94).[5] This disavowal of the viscous and fragmented interior of the body seems to be what Orlan wants to expose and to write into the 'new mirror stage' she refers to in her carnal art manifesto; elsewhere in the same document she refers to it as 'a sort of negation of the mirror stage', which is perhaps a more accurate description of what this opening of the bodily interior proposes. Looking into the entrails reveals an irremediably fragmented body composed of organs, tissue and muscle; it is as if the act of cutting open the body – the gesture of surgery *par excellence* – instantly punctures and deflates the balloon-like 'imaginary body' or 'skin-ego' to which the infant subject starts to attach so much importance in the mirror stage, and which underpins subsequent development of the ego.

These two opposing perceptual experiences that make up the drama of the mirror stage – on the one hand, the reassuring jubilatory pleasure of recognizing (for the first time) one's mirrored body image as one's own, and on the other, the disturbing, chaotic feelings produced by awareness of the uncoordinated 'body-in-bits-and-pieces' (Elizabeth Grosz's phrase) – together seem to add up to what carnal art wants to make visible. In other words, to comprehend the sense of Orlan's reference to 'a new mirror stage', it is important to grasp that this key moment of psychological development in Lacanian theory does not consist solely of the subject's self-aggrandizing and comforting self-positioning on a fictive line of identity that (for Lacan)

---

5. As the work of artists such as Stelarc and Mona Hatoum has shown, the inside of the body contains innumerable scenes and landscapes which are only now becoming visible, thanks to developments in medical imaging technology. Stelarc has done work involving endoscopy, and Hatoum's work 'Corps étranger' (Foreign Body) exposed the spectator to images of the inside of her body taken by a minute camera inserted into a number of different orifices. 'Corps étranger' was also accompanied by a memorable soundtrack of the heaving, breathing activity of the body's interior. Theorist Donna Haraway has observed the equation of Outer (astronomical) Space and Inner (bodily) Space made official in the 100-year history of the National Geographic Society, and comments: 'The final chapter, full of stunning biomedical images, is titled "Inner Space" and introduced with the epigraph, "The Stuff of the Stars Has Come Alive". The photography convinces the viewer of the fraternal relation of inner and outer space. But curiously, in outer space, we see spacemen fitted into explorer craft or floating about as individuated cosmic fetuses, while in the supposed earthy space of our own interiors, we see non-humanoid strangers who are the means by which our bodies sustain our integrity and individuality, indeed our humanity in the face of a world of others' (Haraway 1992b: 320).

corresponds to ego-formation, but is a conflictual drama, as Elizabeth Grosz's account of the mirror stage emphasizes by quoting from Lacan's paper on aggressivity.

> What I have called the *mirror stage* is interesting in that it manifests the effective dynamism by which the subject originally identifies himself with the visual *Gestalt* of his own body: in relation to the still very profound lack of co-ordination of his own motility, it represents an ideal unity, a salutory *imago*; it is invested with all the original distress resulting from the child's intra-organic and relational discordance during the first six months (Lacan 1977: 19, quoted in Grosz 1990: 40–1).

Another presentation of the violence and discord of bodily experience in the mirror stage is made by Elizabeth Wright in her commentary on Samuel Beckett's play *Not I*, infamous for its staging of the 'fragmented body', since the actor's mouth is the only object and image seen. As Wright emphasizes, the genesis of the ego that occurs at the mirror stage is a traumatic as well as a positive and constructive moment because it is 'the primordial moment when the body senses its split from the Real' (Wright 1984: 113). In Lacan's trio of key concepts Imaginary, Symbolic and Real, the Real is the order into which the child is born that precedes any organization of the drives; it is 'anatomical, natural [. . .] (nature in the sense of resistance rather than positive substance), a pure plenitude or fullness' (Grosz 1990: 34). The first wresting away from the sense of organic unity with the world experienced by the child in the Real happens at the mirror stage, which thereby becomes a traumatic event that can return later 'as the experience of the fragmented body, unique for every subject, remainder and reminder of this fracture, appearing in art as images of grotesque dismemberment – Lacan cites Bosch' (Wright 1984: 113). The unconscious phantasy of the fragmented body, with its memory of the disunity and dismemberment felt during its earliest stages of development, thus haunts the individual, returning in dreams or at transformative moments in analysis. Lacan in fact draws attention in his paper on the mirror phase to how signs of malaise in the first months of life betray a psychic 'dehiscence' or 'primordial Discord' that can erupt at any moment later in the individual's life, or in his/her artistic or literary output, and identifies this unrest with disturbances in the relationship with reality (its environment) that the organism establishes through the mirror stage *imago* (Lacan 1977: 4). His association of the portraiture of Bosch and surrealist art such as the dolls of Hans Bellmer with the fragmented body whose materiality and resistance to totalization underlies the mirror stage and the subsequent Imaginary order offers a striking parallel with the 'new mirror stage' or 'sort of negation of the mirror stage' Orlan alludes to in her manifesto of carnal art. For Orlan, the opening-up-to-view of the bodily interior – a kind of substitution of the felt fragmented body for the perfect, unified imaginary body offered to the child's sight in its mirror image – is erotic, and can involve other bodies as well as her own – 'So I can see the heart of my lover and . . . his splendid design has none of the sickly sentimentalities usually drawn . . ./Darling I love your spleen, I love your glottis, I love your pancreas, I love your femur' – it becomes a kind of eroticism of the bodily interior.[6] This unconventional eroticism offsets the more conventional kind seen in her kissing of operating theatre staff at the start of the film of 'Omnipresence'.

Blasphemy is central to Orlan's philosophy of carnal art. Putting Artaud into a humorous context, she states 'To "finish with the judgment of God" we now have epidurals, local anaesthetics and multiple analgesics . . . (long live morphine!)'. But the blasphemy of carnal art goes further than denial and protest against the divine. It functions according to a logic of reversal and transgression; 'Carnal Art transforms the body into language and reverses the Christian principle of the word made flesh into flesh made word' (Orlan 1997: 2). Since the resymbolization of the body will be discussed in detail in a later chapter, I shall limit myself here to carnal art's other targets, of which the two main ones are religion and science. Through the Christian notion of the body as God-given and biological science's discovery of genetic code in DNA respectively, both religion and science dictate that the body we are born with is not to be tampered with. The body, as every human being's personal realm of Nature, represents 'the innate, the inexorable, the programmed' (Orlan 1996: 91). Whereas the main achievement of body artists of the 1960s and 70s was to discover the body as material for representation, carnal art of the 1990s enters into dialogue with scientific and technological advance. For Orlan, DNA 'is our direct rival as far as (sic) artists of representation are concerned' (ibid). Although her cosmetic surgery cannot strictly be said to be modifying her genetic code, her re-imaging of the self to match a computerized design forms a continuum with DNA's status as a modifiable, reprogrammable code.

Rachel Armstrong, qualified in medicine and formerly Orlan's agent, explains the relevance of Orlan's carnal art to medicine by pointing out the parallel between the demise of religion and the rising influence of medicine in contemporary society. It is the medical profession that provides the pastoral care for which people previously looked to the Church and to their local

6. Remarks by Orlan in her own translation, for exhibition 'This Is My Body . . . This Is My Software', Zone Photographic Gallery, Newcastle, UK, 11–26 May 1996.

community, and in the face of the new demands placed upon them, doctors depend increasingly on technology for legitimation of their knowledge. Orlan's surgical project draws attention to the comparable power structures of medicine and religion as institutions. Armstrong also sees Orlan's advertised consciousness throughout her surgery as useful publicity for changing practices in anaesthesia that are altering the doctor-patient relationship in contemporary medicine. More minor and easier surgical interventions mean that a local anaesthetic is now often preferred to a general one. Technology is enabling the conscious participation of the patient in surgery upon his/her body, transforming the 'old nineteenth century hierarchy of omnipotent physicians and passive patients' (Armstrong 1996: 2). The encouragement of activity on the part of the patient is part of a new, more wholistic ethic of medical practice which allows the patient greater involvement in non-urgent surgery, but also expects responsible participation in preparation for and aftercare of the treatment. According to Armstrong, 'The body is the most immediate locus of control and has, thus become a metaphor which has been used as a statement of personal self-identification. Physical protests may be interpreted as an individual assertion of personal freedom in a society which has lost its faith in authority. People are demanding the right to their bodies from the politicians, advertising corporations, beauty industries and the medical profession' (ibid.: 5)

Carnal art is Orlan's term, but its usage might justifiably be extended to a new alliance between art and medicine that has spread through photography, art gallery bookshops and television documentaries in the 1990s. More sophisticated and powerful medical imaging technology enables the production of images of the human body magnified to a level never before seen, and the practice of looking at medical images *as* art reconnects art and medicine, marking a kind of return to sixteenth- and seventeenth-century anatomy lessons, which were given as performances in theatres in the round accompanied by music, with the patient's body fully on view to spectators. (Contemporary history of medicine has observed how the post-Renaissance surrender of the body to medical technicians and professionals opened up a gulf between science and art.) Pre-Renaissance anatomy lessons and illustrations in anatomical textbooks displayed a fascination with the hidden interior of the body which the 1990s began to rediscover. Orlan is one performance artist whose work can be understood as reclaiming the body for art from medical science, or, more interestingly, as reviving a relationship between aesthetic appreciation and scientific comprehension which became lost in modernity's formation of rigid disciplines of study.[7]

7. *The South Bank Show*, 5 April 1998.

It can be argued, then, that carnal art is a thoroughgoing critique of different institutions – of religion, as is shown by Orlan's costumed pastiches of Catholic iconography discussed in Chapter 1, and also of science and medicine. I shall explore the technological futurism of Orlan's art practice further in the next chapter, and look in more detail at readings that have been made of her critique of cosmetic surgery and the beauty industry in Chapter 4. To follow on from my focus on the 'flesh spectacle' that dominates Orlan's carnal art programme, the rest of this chapter will be devoted to discussion of the spectatorship of carnal art.

Looking on in Horror

When presenting her surgical work at conferences, in galleries, and in interviews to newspapers and journals, Orlan has more than once insisted that it is 'harder' on the viewer than it is on her. She does not suffer on the operating table: 'I am not a masochist'. Are hierarchical power relations, or sadomasochistic dynamics, a useful way of understanding Orlan's relationship with the spectators of her surgical work? A view which meets with broad agreement among the many intrigued by 'Reincarnation' is that a barely concealed aggression is implied in the act of having herself operated upon precisely in order to display her cut and bruised body to others. The full colour post-operative plates from the 1993 operation-performance 'Omnipresence' are the main reference here: images of live surgery choreographed as performance art were the first – and major – innovation of 'Reincarnation', but the exhibition of a stage of the cosmetic surgery process that never normally meets the the public eye, let alone an art gallery, is, it can be argued, just as striking a shift in what is acceptable as photographic art. It is also a blatant transgression of a medical taboo.[8]

Jim McClellan wittily sums up Orlan's reversal of the romantic stereotype of the suffering artist in his description of a presentation of her work she made at London's ICA in 1994: 'You could sense the ICA audience wincing.

---

8. In her 1994 interview to the *Observer* Orlan comments, 'Very many surgeons refuse to work with me, in part because of this. They want to keep that hidden. They want to retain a surgical mystery and only reveal the body once it's perfect'. Her interviewer adds 'Certainly, the post-op pictures of Orlan's bruised, swollen face are troubling, more troubling than the vaguely camp slice and dice of her videos, and go to provide perhaps the strongest evidence that her work does, as she claims, add up to some kind of serious critique' (McClellan 1994: 42). One other artist who has made photographs of herself in the post-operative stage of cosmetic surgery is the American Anne Noggle, in her *Face-lift* series (1975), (Meskimmon 1996: 177–8).

If nothing else, Orlan has succeeded in reversing an old artistic cliché. We're the ones who suffer for her art. She at least has the benefit of local anaesthetic' (McClellan 1994: 40). McClellan's observation of the discomfort of the ICA audience, replicated in most of Orlan's audiences, suggests that there is indeed violence at work in the viewing relations Orlan's performances set up. Her aggression, some of which she admits is still turned back upon herself,[9] is primarily directed outwards to her viewers; there is a kind of visual sadism involved. And associated with it, perhaps, a kind of masochism expected or aimed at in her spectators. Any claim that only spectatorial 'masochists' go to watch Orlan perform would clearly be far too sweeping. Her spectators do not arrange to attend Orlan's presentations thinking only of the pleasurable pain the images on display will afford them, and her audiences are made up as much of the ignorant, curious first-time viewers, and the detachedly intrigued as they are of critically self-aware spectators who have reflected on the dynamic in which they are participating. And of course, staying in the show is no more obligatory than it is in the case of other taboo-breaking visual artists such as Serrano. Orlan has come to expect that a number of people will walk out of any performance or lecture she gives, and comments on the phenomenon to her audience. It is something in which she takes some pleasure, and perhaps some pride. (This was my impression on the first occasion I heard her speak, to the Association of Art Historians in Newcastle, England in April 1996, at a conference whose theme was 'Beauty' and where Orlan had top billing.) My suggestion that Orlan counts to some extent on encouraging the exit of spectators from the performance venue is a reinforcement of the idea that a sadistic impulse is involved in her performances. The sadism in this instance might of course be claimed to be self-defeating – an unsustainable sadomasochistic 'contract' between performer and spectator – since it effectively puts an end to any viewing relationship between them. The contractual character of the viewing dynamics in Orlan's surgical work is an issue I shall return to shortly.

A sadistic dynamic in Orlan's exhibition of the violent and disturbing material in which her surgery deals invites comparison not only with other artists who paint, photograph or perform visceral images of the body, but especially, in my view, with other female performance artists whose sexuality is a vital element of the viewing relationship set up with their audiences. It is arguable to what extent the disgust and revulsion provoked by Orlan's

---

9. 'My work has always been hard on me. It's difficult to sustain because it is a form of aggression against myself. Other people perceive it as a form of aggression against them and are therefore frequently very aggressive towards me. You have to be strong to withstand the reactions I get' (McClellan 1994: 42)

organized display of her flesh on the operating table involves the sexuality of performer and viewer, and depends upon its being female flesh. (Can flesh, human or animal, be gendered? If not, gender is still a significant factor in the types of look invited and commanded by its exhibition.)

Other women performance artists who have explored similar territory include Carolee Schneeman, Gina Pane, and Karen Finley. Schneeman's appearance in 1960s happenings, usually naked, was an exhibition of the female body in the name of sexual freedom, an overtly liberatory and political art in stark contrast to that of her contemporary Gina Pane, whose cutting and wounding of her body in performances such as 'Escalade sanglante' (1971) and 'Azione Sentimentale' (1973) was so strongly masochistic in character that it is difficult to claim for her work an intent to aggress the spectator. Pane's text 'Letter to a (female) stranger' presents her self-wounding as being, on the contrary, 'for the love of you: the other' (Pane 1974: 108). Schneeman's action 'Meat Joy' (1964) was perhaps her most uninhibited celebration of carnality. Schneeman's concern to smash taboos about the exhibition of the naked body finds a closer contemporary parallel in the work of performer Karen Finley, particularly acclaimed for 'The Constant State of Desire', a series of text-based performances which began in New York in 1986. Finley's own view of what made this work unacceptable in the most cosmopolitan places – London, Miami – was that it mixed sex, politics and nakedness and linked these issues to her female specificity. Oppressed and repressed female sexuality found an outlet in 'The Constant State of Desire', whose impact Finley links to an as yet unacknowledged sexuality of violence, to 'womb envy' and to male fear of the feminine (Finley 1996: 254–6).

The performances of Schneeman, Finley and Orlan share a capacity to provoke and to shock, by means of their no-holds-barred display of the flesh. This exhibitionism takes on particular force where the issue is the viewing of these performances; their capacity to shock is attributed to the gender and sexuality of the performers. In a conventional psychoanalytic account of the viewing relations set up by showy, transgressive sexual film or performance, exhibitionism in the performer is matched but also contained and controlled by voyeurism in the viewer. But it is possible too, in a different account of spectatorship, that a voyeuristic gaze does not master the performance being viewed, and that the exhibitionism itself be (paradoxically) sadistic, motivated by a drive to control and master.[10] I would contend that the active exhibitionism going on in much women's performance art is sadistic towards its viewer in this way. Where performance is aggressive spectacle, it

---

10. I am endebted for this insight to Emma Wilson, in a paper on Kieslowski's film *Blanc* given at the 1997 conference 'Performance in French Cultural Studies' (Wilson 1999).

is performative; it enacts a shift in power relations between the sexes (where voyeurism is masculine). The outcome, if the male spectator does not leave the room, is greater equality between masculine and feminine positions in the viewer-viewed relationship.

Before discussing the importance of exhibitionistic female sexuality to women's performance art, I suggested that the concept of masochism could be very useful in understanding the viewing positions constructed by Orlan's performances. In order to explore this suggestion further, and indeed, to reach some provisional conclusions about the nature of the spectatorial activity set up by Orlan's work – those surgical performances and other composed images that appear designed to shock, provoke and aggress – I would like now to turn to a theory of spectatorship formulated by a feminist film critic particularly concerned with sadistic, frightening and violent texts and images. Carol Clover's subject is horror cinema, and in the essay 'The Eye of Horror'[11] she sets out in full a theory of masochistic viewing.

In 'The Eye of Horror' Clover seeks to account for the desires and pleasure of the spectator of horror cinema. Why do movie-goers go to see films that they know in advance will be frightening; in other words, why seek out and deliberately undergo intense and violent cinematic experiences – experiences of images which assault the eye? To explain these apparently perverse desires – which in a literal or clinical sense she is not concerned with is exactly what they turn out to be – Clover advances the concept of 'the reactive gaze'. She sets this against a notion of 'the assaultive gaze' much more familiar in recent film theory, even if that is not the name by which it is usually known. She distinguishes between the assaultive and reactive gazes as follows: 'If the emotional project of the first gaze is to assault, the emotional project of the second is to be oneself assaulted – vicariously' (Clover 1992: 174). Discussing Michael Powell's classic film *Peeping Tom* and its central character Mark, whose triple identification in the film as victim of aggression (at the hands of his father film-maker), aggressor-cameraman, and spectator of his own movies, illustrates the triplet of positions underpinning the masochistic structure Clover takes from *Peeping Tom* to apply to numerous horror films, Clover concludes, 'In that re-view of unpleasure there lies perverse pleasure, for the sight of pain inflicted on others is "enjoyed masochistically by the subject through his identification of himself with the suffering object"' (ibid.: 174; Laplanche and Pontalis 1973: 402). The type of looking Clover's 'reactive gaze' describes is not just a kind of failed voyeurism; as she says of Powell's protagonist Mark, 'Mark is more than a failed voyeur; he is a positively

11. *Men, Women and Chainsaws: Gender in the Modern Horror Film* (BFI Publishing, 1992), pp. 166–230. My thanks to Emma Wilson for this highly fruitful reference.

successful masochist' (Clover 1992: 179). The 'victim position' is his aim, spectatorially and ultimately all too really (Mark impales himself upon the phallic-sadistic spike of his own tripod camera, the very instrument with which he has threatened earlier victims).[12]

Clover's concept of the reactive gaze seems irresistibly relevant to the viewing of Orlan's performance practice, as well as to the work of other contemporary body artists and visual artists dealing in graphic or uncompromising images of the human body. Parallels between the visuals of horror film and images of the 'Reincarnation' project spring easily to mind – the photographic plate of a second 'mouth' cut under Orlan's jaw and the double mouths of the *Alien* monsters. The bloody images of the open body and surgical procedures shown in the large photographs of 'Omnipresence' resemble the 'splatter' genre of horror movies more than incidentally. If the spectators of horror film wish or need to review their own past pain through vicarious identification with on-screen victims, can the same dynamics not apply to the viewing of Orlan's photographs and performances from the operating theatre? Horror cinema as Clover theorizes it does not just depict 'hurt' its spectators may already be familiar with according to a kind of 'reflection' model of representation; it actually constructs with its audiences viewing relations that incorporate the experience of being the victim of (sadistic) aggression. *Peeping Tom* shows that its director Michael Powell 'understands the "hurt" to preexist the movie, but he regards it as the cruel business of the horror industry to locate such "hurts" and mine them for their masochistic possibilities' (ibid.: 199).

According to Clover, different sub-genres of horror film – werewolf stories, 'possession' films, slasher movies – appear to be organized around different fears, such as being eaten by an animal, 'being copulated with and giving birth' (the 'possession' film) and thoughts of beating. What they often have in common, and share with war and action films, is a serial narrative made up of repeated episodes of threat, fear and pain. (These episodes are often linked together internally by the 'suspense factor' identified by Theodor Reik

12. Clover develops the notion of the reactive gaze in readings of a number of other horror films. Of Alfred Hitchcock's classic *Psycho*, for example, she notes how the notorious shower scene of Marion Crane's murder 'lasts forty seconds and is composed of as many shots: a rapid-fire concatenation of images' which constitutes 'a breath-taking piece of cinematic violence – and as much at the editorial as at the diegetic level' (Clover 1992: 203). The viewer's eye can literally 'be physically assaulted by the projected image – by sudden flashes of light, violent movement [. . .], fast-cut or exploded images. These are the stock-in-trade of horror' (ibid.: 202–3).

as an important component of masochistic sexuality.)[13] Horror cinema is all about 'scary stories endlessly repeated' – repeated within individual films as well as from film to film. The dominance of repetition in horror 'stands as a narrative manifestation of the syndrome of repetition compulsion', the Freudian notion Clover glosses as follows:

> Defined as an 'ungovernable process originating in the unconscious', whereby a person 'deliberately places himself in distressing situations, thereby repeating an old [but unremembered] experience', repetition compulsion thus has its roots in unpleasure. The function and effects of repetition compulsion are not clear [. . .] What *is* clear is that where there is *Wiederholungszwang* there is historical suffering – suffering that has been more or less sexualized as 'erotogenic masochism'. (ibid.: 213)[14]

For Clover, the compulsively repetitive narratives and codes of horror movies are in themselves evidence that those viewing them are acquainted with 'historical suffering', albeit unconsciously. The cinematic spectator of horror may not be aware of why s/he is so drawn to, and drawn into, the serially episodic 'scare' structure of horror cinema, but this actually reinforces Clover's assertion that such spectators stay with these films' repetitive narratives because of their unconscious masochistic inclination repeatedly to review fear and suffering they themselves have experienced, and 'more or less sexualized'.

There are some telling comparisons between this part of Clover's discussion of the narrative repetition and masochistic spectatorship of horror cinema and the structure of 'The Reincarnation of Saint Orlan'. 'Reincarnation' was from its outset planned as a serial project, which would comprise multiple operations on Orlan's body and facial features. Although the nine operations have featured different body parts and styles of performance, repetition has also been a vital feature of the work. The recycling of images in different media underpins the décor of the operating theatre as Orlan designs it on each occasion. New costumes are mixed with multimedia displays and projections of Orlan's earlier costumed performances and actions. After 'introducing' her key reading texts by Kristeva, Lemoine-Luccioni and Serres,

13. See 'Masochism in Modern Man', Part Two of *Of Love and Lust: On the Psychoanalysis of Romantic and Sexual Emotions* (London: Souvenir Press Ltd, 1975). The suspense element is discussed in pp. 221–35.

14. Clover's sources here are Laplanche and Pontalis, *The Language of Psychoanalysis*, entry on 'Compulsion to Repeat', p. 78; Edward Bibring, 'The Conception of the Repetition Compulsion'; Laplanche, *Life and Death in Psychoanalysis*, pp. 85–102; Sigmund Freud, *Beyond the Pleasure Principle* and 'The Economic Problem of Masochism'.

Orlan has re-used them or parts of them in subsequent operations. Repetition and recycling of material is, in sum, essential to 'Reincarnation'. The interested viewer of the images generated by Orlan's surgical work must be predisposed to subject him/herself to serial representations of the horror cinema type, where single films and groups of films are structured by repeated episodes. In dwelling on how Clover's theory of viewing horror can elucidate Orlan's surgical practice, I am not suggesting, though, that the two fit so snugly that we should consider 'Reincarnation' a cultural equivalent of horror cinema. To do that would prejudge the issue of what place Orlan's practice occupies in a hierarchy of art above popular culture, a particularly fluid question in performance of recent decades.[15] One obvious difference between 'Reincarnation''s structure and the codes of commercial horror cinema is the diminished role of narrative and the absence of a certain ending to Orlan's project, an issue I shall discuss further in Chapter 4.

'Art is a Dirty Job . . .'

In discussing the spectatorship of Orlan's art practice up to this point, I have suggested that sadomasochism implicit in the viewing relations of her performances runs just one way. It is Orlan's display of her body which is sadistic, as well as exhibitionistic, to the viewer who masochistically stands in a gallery, lecture hall or other public space where s/he 'suffers' Orlan's images in a kind of reactive passivity. This reading of the violent viewing relations of shocking and provocative art does not address any dynamic running in the contrary direction, when the reversibility of sadomasochism's active-passive polarity and its violence is, after all, a central feature of the relationships that characterize it. With this reversibility in view, I shall now broach two questions: what sadism, if any, remains in the spectator's gaze upon Orlan's open, cut or bruised body, and is it at all helpful to consider Orlan herself as a masochist?

Orlan has herself pronounced, on more than one occasion, that she is *not* a masochist. Many of the images from 'Omnipresence' show her laughing in the operating theatre, and smiling with apparent pleasure as the scalpel cuts away at her face. Central to the blasphemous reversal of Christianity in Orlan's carnal art is its promotion of pleasure and denial of the suffering of the flesh so frequently thematized in Christian, and especially Catholic, texts and art. Her manifesto of carnal art states:

15. Auslander, 'Going with the Flow: Performance Art and Mass Culture', *TDR: a journal of performance studies* Vol 33 No. 2 (Summer 1989), 119–36.

Unlike 'Body Art', Carnal Art does not seek pain, does not confront it as a source
of purification, and does not conceive it as redemption [. . .] Carnal Art judges the
famous 'You will give birth in pain' to be anachronistic and ridiculous [. . .] now
we have epidurals and multiple anaesthetics as well as analgesics, long live
morphine! Down with pain! (Orlan 1997: 2)

The only pain surgery causes her is when she too looks at the images her
operations have generated: 'I am sorry to make you suffer, but remember, I
am not suffering, except like you, when I look at the images' (Orlan 1995:
6). But this non-identification with the literal (rather than spectatorial) victim
position is contradicted in the same article-interview:

A few words on pain. I am trying to make this work the least masochistic possible,
but there is a price to be paid for the anaesthetic injections are not at all pleasurable!
(I prefer to be drinking champagne or a good wine with my friends rather than
being operated on!) And yet, everybody experiences this, it's like going to the dentist,
you grimace for a few seconds . . . There are of course several injections and so
several grimaces . . . After the operations it is more or less uncomfortable and more
or less painful, and so I take analgesics like everyone else (ibid.: 10)

Two elements of this admission deserve comment, in my view. The first is
that it is more than a passing irony that the painful stage of Orlan's operations
is the anaesthetic injections intended to insulate her from the pain of the
surgeon's knife. The type of anaesthetic administered to Orlan is an epidural
block, which involves an injection of anaesthetic into the space outside the
'dura mater' enveloping the spinal cord. It is in itself a risky procedure –
perhaps the element of Orlan's surgery that invites closest comparison with
the overt play with risk in the performances of 1960s and 1970s body artists
(Chris Burden's 'Shoot'). In saying that these injections are not just risky,
but painful too, Orlan exposes the apparently inevitable logic of suffering
implied in her surgical project; the very procedure that affords her the
conscious participation essential to the choreographing of her operations *as*
performances is the one which causes her pain. The administration of the
anaesthetic is a kind of marginalium to the operation-performance itself,
but it is this marginal or borderline element which exposes Orlan's affir-
mations of pain-free surgery as ultimately untenable.

The second noteworthy element of Orlan's admission to suffering is her
casual comparison of her epidurals to a dentist's injections. What is most
revealing about the comment is not the disavowal, which is common in
Orlan's presentations of her surgical work and in itself suggests a certain
masochism, but her insistence on the ordinary nature of the pain involved
('everybody experiences this'). In presenting her elective suffering as everyday,

Orlan identifies with a pain known to her public. The dentist's surgery and the operating theatre share their status as sites of the medical institution, but most people's experience of injections is limited to those the dentist administers. The public she is addressing is, as she says herself, 'a public not necessarily involved in the microcosm of art' (ibid.: 9).

A further, more important masochistic dimension of Orlan's surgical project I would point to was suggested to me by Kathy O'Dell's important article 'The Performance Artist as Masochist Woman' (O'Dell 1988). O'Dell addresses many of the issues that link masochism to performance, including Reik's exploration of the demonstrative factor as one of the 'four ingredients of masochism' (ibid.: 97). (The other three 'ingredients' are fantasy, suspense and provocation.) O'Dell's highly convincing reading of the performances of Gina Pane and Ulrike Rosenbach as masochistic uses Freud's notion of 'feminine masochism' from 'The Economic Problem of Masochism', as well as the Brechtian concepts of 'distance' and alienation. She also refers to another theory of masochism that she does not link to the performances of Pane and Rosenbach – Gilles Deleuze's 'Masochism: An Interpretation of Coldness and Cruelty'. As O'Dell sees it, Deleuze

> has extended the Reikian lists to include a pseudo-legal notion of 'contract', or the prerequisite of an agreement between masochist and sadist. This ingredient is especially important to recognize in that it attests to the masochist's desire to operate *in* society, which is to say, to operate within and to (possibly) criticize institutionality, exemplified here by the institution of law. (ibid.: 97)

Recent discussion of masochism's role in artistic production has focused on how such a contractual sadomasochism might be constructed. The concept seems particularly important to women artists, writers and film-makers, in view of masochism's traditional association with the feminine, and feminism's criticism of patriarchal institutionality, and re-evaluation of women's position within society. If the demonstrative dimension of masochism identified by Reik and explored by O'Dell is at work within the realm of women's art, how is it linked into society, and to what extent does it function independently of sadists? Are sadists necessary to masochists? This last question re-opens a long-standing debate within psychoanalysis about the primacy of masochism over sadism, an idea Deleuze supports (the chapter 'Psychoanalysis and the Problem of Masochism' in *Masochism* explicitly entertains 'doubts about the unity and intercommunication of sadism and masochism'(Deleuze 1989: 109)[16]), and one with which feminists have tended to agree. O'Dell's view

16. Gilles Deleuze, *Masochism*, trans. Jean McNeil (New York: Zone Books, 1989), pp. 103–10 (p. 109). Originally published as 'Le Froid et le Cruel', in *Présentation de Sacher-Masoch* (Paris: Editions de Minuit, 1967).

of Freud's tendency throughout his work to emphasize the primacy of sadism over masochism is that it is a perverse theory (O'Dell 1988: 96).

Deleuze's understanding of masochism as contractual, and as harbouring within it a critique of society and institutionality – he distinguishes contract and law, stating that the terms of masochistic contracts become increasingly strict until they give way to and are invalidated by the law (ibid.: 92) – is particularly relevant to one aspect of Orlan's 'Reincarnation' project. This is the end Orlan envisages for the project, the final stage following the final operation, in which she will apply for a new artistic *and* legal identity.

> When the operations are finished, I will employ an advertising agency to find me a first and second name and an artist's name, then I will get a lawyer to appeal to the Public Prosecutor to accept my new identities with my new face. *This is a performance inscribed within the social fabric, a performance which goes as far as the law . . . as far as a complete change of identity* (Orlan 1995: 10, my emphasis).

Orlan's surgical self-transformation will for most of its duration have had little to do with the law, although much to do with institutionality, as I (and she) have argued. But the final stage of 'Reincarnation' she has planned comprises a full-scale address to the organs of the State in France, involving the Public Prosecutor as well as her own lawyers. Orlan is relaxed about the outcome of this extraordinary appeal, commenting that if it fails, it will nonetheless constitute 'part of the work', an artistic rather than a politico-juridical part. The planned extension of 'Reincarnation' as far as legal process and the State brings Orlan's project into the realm of a masochism no longer directly related to the infliction of pain upon the self, Deleuze's contractual dimension. If Orlan's surgery has a limited amount to do with masochism in the sexual sense of the term, it can claim particular kinship with masochism's sociopolitical dimension. As O'Dell says of performance artists Pane and Rosenbach, 'by forcing the issue of masochism to the performance level, the artists we are discussing trigger a questioning of the whole structure of masochism from the world of fantasy (which includes all visual matter, all art) on up through the contractual (which pulls each and every one of us into the picture) (O'Dell 1988: 97).

If a type of masochism can after all be acknowledged to be at work in 'Reincarnation', what of the sadism that may reside in the gaze at images of Orlan on the operating table? Other women performance artists who have played overtly with the sadistic impulses of their spectators come to mind here. A performance piece by Marina Abramovic in 1974 consisted of her lying dressed in a Naples gallery, with the invitation extended to her spectators to use instruments placed nearby according to their wishes. This performance was part reprise, part extension of Yoko Ono's 'Cut Piece', first done in Kyoto in 1964. In both performances, the artists' clothes were ripped and removed by onlookers, and in Abramovic's her skin was also slashed (Goldberg 1995: 165).

Sadism is much more commonly assumed to be a component of the look than is masochism; Carol Clover develops her concept of the reactive gaze against a notion of the assaultive gaze long dominant in theories of spectatorship. Christian Metz and Laura Mulvey's enormously influential theories of the voyeuristic cinematic gaze held sway in post-1970s film theory in as masterful a way as the camera they write about, and have only quite recently been challenged. Clover's deconstruction of the Metz-Mulvey axis of gaze theory builds on the work of critics such as Kaja Silverman, whose reading of Powell's *Peeping Tom*, for example, exposes voyeurism as a 'by nature unachievable' *fantasy* of phallic mastery (Clover 1992: 179; Silverman 1988: 32-41). In 'The Eye of Horror', Silverman's Lacanian emphasis on the difference between imaginary and symbolic relationships to the phallus (the fantasy of phallic mastery takes place in the imaginary register, for any subject, whatever his/her position vis-à-vis the axis of sexual difference) gives way to a post-Lacanian reading of horror cinema in which 'assaultive gazing never prevails' (Clover 1992: 187). The sub-genre Clover draws on in this part of her analysis is the slasher film, self-evidently a locus of sadistic violence against women. Claiming that what these films illustrate is the violent potential – visual as well as actual – of their male characters' falling-short of phallic mastery ('when men cannot perform sexually, they stare and kill instead'), Clover concludes 'slasher killers are by generic definition sexually inadequate – men who kill precisely because they *cannot* fuck' (ibid.: 186). Whatever the 'successful' murder tally of the slasher killer, a 'remarkably durable theme of horror involves turning the assaultive gaze back on itself' (ibid.: 187) – and this 'turning back' or failing of the assaultive gaze occurs in a confrontation with the feminine. How the dynamics of this confrontation apply to the viewing of Orlan's work will be the subject of the final section of this chapter.

'The Devil Himself Flees...'

Orlan's contribution to an international art symposium held in Aix-la-Chapelle in 1978 was a performance entitled 'Documentary Study: The Head of Medusa'.

> This involved showing my sex (of which half my pubic hair was painted blue) through a large magnifying glass – and this, during my period. Video monitors showed the heads of those arriving, those viewing, and those leaving. Freud's text

on the 'Head of Medusa' was handed out at the exit, stating: "At the sight of the vulva even the devil runs away" (Orlan 1996: 84).

A description of this performance from another source supplies the information that before seeing Orlan's magnified sex, spectators encountered a huge four-metre high canvas onto which was stretched and pinned one of her trousseau sheets, daubed with touches of yellow and blue paint and a red substance that was in fact her blood. It was through a hole in the centre of this canvas that viewers looked at Orlan, whose pubic hair was brushed with yellow as well as blue paint. The whole installation was a 'vision machine' recalling Marcel Duchamp's famous last work the 'Etant donné' (Ceysson 1990: 15).

Her performance of Medusan femininity was one of two works in which Orlan has deliberately invoked a mythical or literary 'monstrous' woman. This witty and yet potentially taboo-breaking performance, the display of her bleeding vagina, was inspired by a famous twentieth-century intertext to the Medusa myth, Freud's short essay of 1922, 'Medusa's Head'. Here Freud offers his rather unliterary interpretation of the enduring power of the Medusa, which is that her decapitated head is a symbol for the terrifying, castrated genitals of the woman/Mother. The essay is a classic example of the visual phallocentrism of Freudian psychoanalysis, according to which the penis is the desirable organ, while the woman's genitals are either hidden from view altogether, or too disgusting to set eyes upon. Woman can be construed as castrated only on the information provided by vision. Orlan's performance appears to have been a direct allusion and challenge to the phallocentric representations of the sexed body found in Freud's writings, and concentrated in 'Medusa's Head'.

Speaking about her performance practice, Orlan has said she aims to resist the kind of modernist reading of art according to which form exceeds content in importance, and art practice is in the grip of incessantly advancing formal innovation.[17] 'Documentary Study. The Head of Medusa' stands out amongst Orlan's performance pieces as having particularly powerful content, while also being crucially concerned with the means of representation of that content, with viewing and the challenge to a certain type of look. As is indicated by the video monitors that reflected back the spectator's gaze, his/her involvement in this scene of representation is every bit as important as the role of the performer. (This is also the case in Freud's essay, where it is the Medusa's ability to turn those who dared to look upon her to stone that allows him to interpret the spectator's terrified reaction – he is 'stiff with

17. In conversation with me in Paris, August 1998.

terror' – as the stiffness of a consoling erection, consoling because the spectator is comforted by the knowledge that he still possesses the penis the Medusa/woman lacks.) The aspect of Orlan's performance which reveals that it was intended as self-reflexive work upon representation is a negative one; her invocation of the myth of the Medusa was not an impersonation. Where the myth, and Freud's essay, zoom in on the Medusa's monstrous head, Orlan chose the body. Rather than simulating the horrifying visage and snakes-for-hair common to representations of the mythological Medusa, Orlan's performance used its literal, demetaphorized referent, the vulva. The expression 'Documentary Study' in the title of her performance (written on the canvas through which spectators peeped) indicates that she was working upon the real, and, as the documentary genre does, on the way that specific sight/site of the real may be represented. Nothing in the performance confirmed Freud's metaphor, Medusa's head = female genitals; rather, it worked against that equivalence, in the effort to undo it, and ask what alternative means of representing female sexuality are available to contemporary art practice.

One writer who has recently turned her attention to representations of monstrous femininity is the feminist film critic Barbara Creed, in *The Monstrous Feminine: Film, Feminism, Psychoanalysis*. To close this chapter, I shall follow Creed's lead in taking 'excessive' images of the feminine in order to challenge the representational frameworks according to which femininity is read and understood.

The main emotion felt by the (male) spectator in the imaginary drama of gaze and display Freud describes in 'Medusa's Head' is castration anxiety. Orlan's re-enactment of this drama may be read as a confrontational, but also knowing and fun-poking mise-en scène of castration anxiety. In *The Monstrous Feminine*, Creed suggests that horror may be distinguished from other film genres by the way it does not attempt to soothe castration anxiety. Multiple representations of female monstrosity are one means it uses to arouse and play on the spectator's fears; 'the monstrous-feminine constitutes an important and complex stereotype which can be broken down into a number of different figures of female horror; woman as archaic mother, monstrous womb, vampire, possessed monster, *femme castatrice*, witch, castrating mother' (Creed 1993: 151–2). Unlike Carol Clover, who explores the type of look set up by the cinematic apparatus and narrative structures of horror films, Creed concentrates mainly on the question of what the relationship of gender is to the viewing position that is constructed by images of the monstrous-feminine. In so doing, she seeks to deconstruct phallocentric theories of looking. Her subject is horror cinema, but she argues that the aesthetic and ideological structures of encounters with the monstrous-feminine are present in the legends and myths of all ages and across the cultural spectrum. From the Medusa to the *Alien* films, in poetry and in pornography, representations of the monstrous-feminine expose the construction of phallocentric looking, as it is only by repressing certain important aspects of these representations that this look can pretend to master its female object. Female monsters of myth, fairy tale and popular fiction challenge phallocentric representations of woman because the monstrous-feminine does not fit within the phallocentric Symbolic order. Looking at the monstrous-feminine requires an alternative theory of what that look consists of.

Creed's argument makes direct reference to Freud's essay on the Medusa's head. She maintains that the fundamental mistake of phallocentric theories of looking is to have neglected woman's role as castrator – for Freud, although castration is (he claims) an actuality for the little girl, and operates as a threat for the little boy, this threat emanates from the father, never from the mother. In Lacan's move away from the biologism of Freud's accounts of infantile sexuality to a linguistic and symbolic understanding of castration, the mother is, similarly, not a punitive figure in her own right, but invokes the Father's authority (the 'Law of the Father within her' (Grosz 1990: 70)) on loan in order to punish or threaten the child. According to Creed, it is the Freudo-Lacanian suppression of the castrating woman in favour of the castrated woman that leads to the psychoanalytic presentation of female sexuality as passive, rather than active.

Creed's turn to the concept of the *femme castratrice* raises questions for (feminist) commentators seeking to explore representations (such as Orlan's Medusa study) that deal directly in images of phallicity and castration. Creed in fact singles out Freud's concept of the phallic woman, the powerful mother figure as she is fantasized by the child passing through the different stages of infantile sexuality, for criticism, seeing it as a necessary precursor to his view of all women as castrated. Asking of woman 'Is she or isn't she castrated?' led Freud to the concept of the phallic woman/mother, whereas if he had asked 'Is woman castrated or does she castrate?' the doors would have been (re-)opened to the concept of the castrating woman/mother, and to the understanding of female sexuality as active. A representation of powerful, aggressive femininity can accommodate both concepts, meaning that they are often confused; Creed finds examples of loose use of the term 'phallic woman' in Laplanche and Pontalis, and comments interestingly on women artists' use of images of phallic women, which can be observed in many domains of representation, from drawing, through photography to pornography.

For Creed's argument in her chapter about the use of stereotypes of monstrous femininity to represent images of castration, the phallic and the castrating woman are two incompatible archetypes of femininity: 'the former ultimately represents a comforting phantasy of sexual sameness, and the latter a terrifying phantasy of sexual difference' (Creed 1993: 158). For the more deconstructively inclined feminist critic this incompatibility is questionable, since both concepts very clearly still endorse the logic of castration ('having it or not having it') and the framework of Oedipal authority always ultimately revelatory of the phallocentrism of psychoanalysis. Do feminist critics of images of women want to endorse the *femme castatrice* as their main or only representation of active female sexuality? Orlan's Medusa study is evidently indissociable from myths and archetypes of castration, but the performance was too knowing, too self-reflexive in its architecture to straightforwardly endorse just one image of active feminine sexuality such as the castrating woman. Where Creed's analysis of the monstrous-feminine is valuable, though, is because it pinpoints precisely those aspects of female sexuality to which Orlan's Medusa study drew attention. Firstly, its active nature; the active, creative consciousness of the female artist who had conceived this conceptual performance was as present in it as the explicit body challenging the spectator's look, and indeed, inseparable from that body. Secondly, the performance openly flouted the taboo on menstruation, one of the most ingrained cultural taboos concerning feminine sexuality. A phenomenon still prevailing in many tribal non-Western societies, the menstruation taboo is not without its effects upon the cultural imagery of the developed Western world, where menstrual blood is rarely seen (it does not appear in advertising for women's sanitary products), and even more rarely displayed. A third aspect of feminine sexuality occluded by Freud in his scenes of the perception of sexual difference is the difference between the genitals of little girls and those of women, more likely to be hidden in pubic hair (ibid.: 113–4). Orlan's performance, with her painted pubic hair, must certainly have left her viewers in no doubt that they were looking at the genital organs of an adult woman.

Orlan's performance of Medusan femininity referred to exactly those elements of female sexuality ignored by Freud in his determination to present women as castrated. The imaginary castrating woman is not a sight the Freudian spectator can safely behold, which is why the explanations of gazing upon the Medusa Freud offers in 'Medusa's Head' are all unsatisfactory. (The first is a recourse to homosexuality, in which Freud suggests that the Medusa myth originates in Greek culture because 'the Greeks were in the main strongly homosexual'. In the second, where the onlooker's dread is described, Freud takes immediate refuge in the familiar logic of castration ('stiffening' indicates an erection); in the third, the idea that the genitals (female or male) may have an apotropaic function (i.e. they serve to ward off aggressors) leads Freud to contemplate the spectator's flight from the scene ('We read in Rabelais of how the Devil took to flight when the woman showed him her vulva' (Freud 1922: 274) – the printed words handed out to Orlan's spectators.) Viewers of her performance may not actually have retreated or run away, but the cameras set up to film them showed them their reactions in live playback, dwelling playfully on their anxiety about their viewing rather than seeking to assuage it, a joke at the expense of the Freudian spectator.

Apotropaic after a fashion, Orlan's display of her vulva alluded to a castration that was not literal (the 'feminine' kind of castration found in Freudian theory), but symbolic; a castration (in Lacanian terms a feminization) of the look. To the male-identified viewer, Orlan's vulva/vagina became an 'oeil-sexe', a look back at the gaze attempting mastery. In Carol Clover's terms, the performance showed that the sadistic-voyeuristic gaze at the woman persists, but does not ultimately prevail. The plots of Clover's horror movies show time and again an aspiration to phallic mastery that is followed by a failure to master the woman as object of the look. What appear to be 'femme fatale' stories, in which the feminine object is identified as deathly and enigmatic, can be read more subtly as illustrations of 'overzealous male gazing' in which '[a]t best, it seems, assaultive gazing is risky business' (Clover 1992: 189). The reaction of women spectators to Orlan's performance may have been rather different – and difficult to second-guess. What the 'Documentary Study' would seem to have offered its female-identified viewers, though, is an opportunity to identify with the monstrous-feminine usually entirely foreclosed on in phallocentric scopic regimes. Any woman voyeuristically objectifying Orlan as the Medusa – 'consuming' her as spectacle as has so often occurred with the colourful and activity-filled images of her on the operating table – would be failing to spot the importance of this possible identification with monstrous femininity, and remaining complicit with the sadistic-voyeuristic male gaze.

Images of monstrous femininity are inadmissable to the male imaginary as they are unviewable by the male gaze. By supplying these horrifying images live, Orlan confronted the male imaginary with its own abjected content. Doing so constituted a provocative performance that advertised the persistence of misogynistic taboos in the Western cultural imaginary, and deconstructed – exposed and revealed to its unsuspecting spectators – the symbolization process that enabled Freud to affirm the Medusa's head as a symbol for the female genitalia in the first place.

Cyborg Women, Posthumanity, and Technological Body Art

My discussion of Orlan's Medusa study in the final part of the last chapter suggested that the extreme content and mode of presentation of this performance worked to force a reorganization, from first principles, of the gendered power relations of viewing. By taking up the position of the monstrous feminine occluded from existing models of spectatorship, Orlan challenges those models, and offers new possibilities of identification to her female spectators. In this chapter, which will assess Orlan's contribution to current debates about the definition and status of being 'human', I shall begin by staying with monsters, whose various, unpredictable and grotesque forms trouble definitions of 'human' and 'humanity'. In subsequent sections of the chapter I shall further this exploration of the status of 'human' in contemporary culture by addressing issues raised by the cyborg body, an identity Orlan has claimed for herself through her work with cosmetic surgery and other body technologies.

Over centuries of human history monsters have acted, as the feminist theorist Nina Lykke suggests, as 'boundary phenomena' between the viewable and the unviewable, between the human and the animal, between socially acceptable and abject bodies (Lykke 1996a: 14). Etymologically, a *monster/ monstrum* is an 'object of display'. As creatures of fable, myth and fairy tale, or exhibits at fairs, sideshows and the circus, it is always their separateness and passive difference that monsters advertise. Their object-status draws attention to what sets them apart from the human onlooker, and so to the boundaries between humanity and its others. The monster's meaning as an 'object of display' immediately raises further questions about the aesthetics of monstrosity. What facial and bodily features count as monstrous? What meanings can be ascribed to these features, and how are these meanings determined?

An important aspect of any consideration of monstrous appearance is the distinction between the body and the face. Deformity can affect any part of the human body, but facial disfigurement seems particularly significant in judgements of what counts as 'monstrous' and what does not. The face is the focal point of Orlan's reconstruction of her identity; Michel Onfray has suggested that for Orlan, 'the answer to the question of identity is the face' (Onfray 1996: 38), and rightly draws attention to the fact that she has not at any point publicized plans for operations on non-facial bodily parts. Orlan's stage-by-stage redesign of her face is the centrepiece of her becoming monstrous: the goddesses' and icons' features she has had sculpted into her face have made it a panoply of allusions, a site of multiple and proliferating meanings. Discord and tension have been generated by the deliberate distortion of a previously well-proportioned face.

In order to draw out the implications of this centrality of the face to 'Reincarnation' and to Orlan's performance of monstrous femininity, I shall first summarize an account of monstrosity by the Lacanian cultural theorist Slavoj Zizek, which ascribes particular importance to the part played by facial features in the constitution of monstrous identities (Zizek 1991). Then, by critiquing the phallocentrism of Zizek's reading, I shall demonstrate how Orlan's redesign of her facial features has appeared to support a Lacanian account of facial monstrosity, in order ultimately to depart from it.

Monsters, Faces and Noses

Zizek's monstrosity theory is a historical one, formulated around modernist and postmodernist ideas of subjectivity. His survey of monstrous figures in the art and literature of the nineteenth and twentieth centuries takes in Maupassant, the stories of Kaspar Hauser and The Flying Dutchman, the paintings of Edvard Munch, films by Hitchcock, and David Lynch's *The Elephant Man*. Monsters are conventionally positioned as the object rather than the subject of literary and film narratives, but how their appearances are read depends on the subject-object relations of the narrative in question, and these subject-object relations are always influenced by social or historical factors.

For Zizek, the Enlightenment stage of modernity marks the onset of a new relationship to the monstrous object or 'other'. To explain this development, he sets Lacan against Kant. Lacan's conception of the ego is that it is a substantial entity, a graspable object or thing, which diametrically opposes it to the formalist, transcendental turn of Kant's thinking on subjectivity. Kant, like other Enlightenment theorists, preserved the unified, rational subject theorized by Descartes, but added to it by de-substantializing subjectivity away from physicality and the body. The effect of this de-substantialization was to transform the symbolic structures through which non-normative subjectivities are generated or suppressed: 'It is this very de-substantialization [of the subject] that opens up the empty space (the "blank surface") onto which fantasies are projected, where monsters emerge!' (ibid.: 66). Monsters are the locus of the substantial content missing from the Enlightenment subject, a positive to the subject's negative. In Lacanian terms, these monsters can be thought of as the 'Thing' (*la Chose*), made of the same stuff as the abject, unsymbolizable materiality of the maternal body. The social misfits and malformed creatures peopling the stories of post-Enlightenment literature are the very embodiment of 'substance' – the unthinking matter which formal, rational, autonomous subjectivity no longer accommodated.

Zizek's aim in formulating this theory is not to analyse particular monster narratives, but to account for the symbolic space in which monsters appear. He explicitly privileges form over content: 'the error of content analysis is to proceed too quickly and to take for granted the fantasy surface itself, the empty form/frame that offers space for the appearance of monstrous content' (ibid.: 63). It is highly significant that his choice of post-Enlightenment monsters includes no females, and this is an aspect of his theory I shall return to particularly when explaining its relevance for Orlan's 'Reincarnation' project. First, I shall look at Zizek's discussion of the text central to his analysis, in which he pursues his Lacanian reading of the features of the monstrous face.

This key text is Gaston Leroux's 1912 novel *The Phantom of the Opera*, a choice Zizek justifies with the unsupported claim that the phantom is 'undoubtedly mass culture's central apparition' (ibid.: 45). Like the other monsters on which his theory is built, the Elephant Man and the homunculus of Edvard Munch's painting 'The Scream', the phantom is male. (Zizek's opening remarks about the different status of paternal authority under modernism and postmodernism indicate that the male monster is, albeit in a complex sense, a paternal figure.) And he is a romantic character; a legend of the Paris opera reputedly possessed of a beautiful singing voice, he was traumatized by his mother's rejection of him in early childhood, exhibited at sideshows as a freak, then later employed by the Shah of Persia for his talents as a warmonger and architect. He is an attractive object of analysis because of the 'repulsive horror' of his face , with its dark, sunken eyes, yellow skin and non-existent nose.

The features of the phantom's face on which Zizek bases his reading are its deformed, distorted contours, and its nose. Morphological uncertainty, which Zizek refers to by the Lacanian term 'anamorphotic distortion', is a reliable characteristic of the monstrous.[1] Post-operative photographs of the bloated features created by cosmetic surgery, such as the decorated, full-colour plates Orlan exhibits, elicit the same simultaneous fascination and disgust as anamorphotic distortion, the locking-together of gaze and object induced by monstrous sights. Zizek's interpretation of the phantom's nose follows a more familiar, Freudian line; Leroux's description 'the *absence* of that nose is a terrible thing to look at' irresistibly encodes the phantom's face as a site of lack, and therefore of femininity. Remaining loyal to the Freudian idea that the child is always to some degree a substitute for the penis the mother lacks, Zizek suggests that the effective absence of a nose from the phantom's face could explain his mother's rejection of him. A television adaptation of the phantom's story reversed the plot of Leroux's novel by having the phantom's mother find him attractive enough to accept and love. Zizek's suggestion that these two versions of the story be read as complementary-if-opposed versions of the same narrative is based on the idea that what the TV mother saw on her child's face was an imaginary phallus, 'in short, the accomplishment of her (maternal) desire to obtain in her child her missing phallus' (ibid.: 47). A straightforward, positive illustration of such a phallus-on-a-face is provided by the Elephant Man, whose huge phallic protuberance on his forehead was the focal point of his ugliness. For both the phantom of the opera and the Elephant Man, deformity is symbolically phallic, and in addition, the misshapen feature is read as the inscription of the maternal gaze onto the surface of the offspring's face.

For Zizek, the notion of phallophany – the 'revealed phallus' – is what distinguishes postmodernist from modernist aesthetics The phallus not yet 'sublated' (*aufgehoben*) into the signifier (the anchor of identification with the paternal symbolic order) is the phallus that remains visible, the maternal phallus. I shall explain shortly how this notion relates to Orlan's facial self-redesign. The other aspect of Zizek's account of monstrosity I first want to draw out is the construction he puts on the influence of the maternal gaze. The examples of the phantom and the Elephant Man ascribe a vital role to the mother-child relationship in the formation of monstrosity; mother and monstrous infant are locked together in an embrace of desiring gazes equipped with a quasi-magical power to shape and sculpt the flesh. This account of the capacity of the maternal gaze to produce monsters recalls the seventeenth-

1. Zizek suggests, interestingly, that reactions to the anamorphotic transformation of the body, such as those provoked by traditional, non-European body modification practices, are culturally specific; 'the crippling of female feet in China, the protraction of the neck of the women of the Padaung of Burma[. . .] can evoke nothing but disgust in a foreign gaze' (Zizek 1991: 68). The boundary separating beauty from disgust varies from one culture to the next.

and eighteenth-century theory of the maternal imagination, according to which strong impressions received by the mother's mind during pregnancy (the products either of fantasy or of sights actually seen) imprinted themselves on the foetus she was carrying (Braidotti 1996b: 145–8). Phallophany is 'a kind of brand attesting that the subject is caught in the desire of the other (mother), entrapped in her dream', or 'struck by the whip of her gaze' (Zizek 1991: 58).

As a type of monstrosity, phallophany offers a tempting reading of the resculpted face Orlan set out to acquire in 1990. A vaunted feature of her self-redesign was a huge, bulbous nose that was to be as large as surgery could construct. The aim of this particular operation appeared to be increased, exaggerated monstrosity, an instantly perceivable deviance from any norms of feminine beauty. It seems now that this operation, which was to take place in Japan, will not go ahead.[2] The interpretation of this change of design I would suggest, following and departing from Zizek's theory of phallophanic monstrosity, is that it reveals Orlan is not (as her original plan suggested) caught in the mirror-prison of mother-daughter relations implied by the Lacanian model. This revelation adds to and reinforces my comments in Chapter 1 about the important influence on her work of Orlan's negative relationship with her (now deceased) mother.

In the early to mid-1990s Orlan spoke of her Japanese 'nose-job' as a kind of climactic conclusion to the 'Reincarnation' project. The construction of a grossly protuding phallic nose would have been readable as the compliant inscription on her body of the desire of the Freudo-Lacanian mother for the phallus. The concept of the phallic woman/mother, as my readings in Chapter 2 have shown, is not usefully appropriable for feminism. As an end-point to 'Reincarnation', the construction of a phallophanic nose would have marked a reneging on the open-ended, experimental identity work which has characterized Orlan's surgical project from the outset. It is nonetheless telling that she envisaged herself with an enormous, rhinoceros-like nose, only to abandon the plan to acquire it. Her change of plan illustrates the double bind of her relationship to phallocentrically organized visual images, which initially acknowledged the representational framework of the phallocentric symbolic order, but has resisted its inscriptions on her flesh. Zizek's aesthetics of monstrosity is organized around the idea of phallophany, and around male monsters, whether as subject or object of the narratives he considers. He at

2. Orlan explains that this is because it has not proved possible to secure suitable medical expertise or other guarantees necessary to the safe execution of the surgery, because her contacts in Japan seem to have lost interest in the idea, and because (most significantly for my reading), it would be a 'surenchère' – a bridge too far, as it were.

no point attempts to account for the narratives and images of monstrous women which hold as important a place in Western cultural history as the modern male monsters he elects to discuss. Orlan's work, by contrast, openly exhibits its double relationship to the 'fantasy space' of modern patriarchy. She plays upon the appeal of its images and sometimes appears to be caught in its snare, but ultimately remains aloof both from its linear, end-stopped temporality, and from the morphology of its images.

The Face and the Human

As the focal point of the monstrous appearance Orlan has acquired since beginning surgery, her face actively questions what it is to look 'human'. Her use of the face as signifier calls knowingly upon centuries of visual representations that have put it at the centre of their enquiry into human identity. Portraiture in painting, the use of photography to exercise power through apparatuses of social control, and the cinematic close-up are all examples of how the face magnifies humanness by concentrating its supposed qualities into its open, contoured surface.

In order to further the investigation of the face as a signifier of humanity, I would like now to turn to the concept of 'faciality' introduced by Gilles Deleuze and Félix Guattari in *A Thousand Plateaus*. At the start of their discussion of faciality (*visagéité*) they state that the face is 'a horror story'; its skin 'façade' conceals a monstrous 'horror' of bloody tissue, muscle and bone. Without skin, the face gives way to the concave spaces and ghoulish grin of the death's head. The face 'proper' is this surface skin-face, but recognizing this entails a different conception of the face from the centuries of representations in which it, like the eye, has been seen as a kind of 'window onto the soul' – a channel leading to the mind and personality of its bearer. Deleuze and Guattari's discourse on faciality works to free the image of the face from this embeddedness in humanist discourse. Eschewing the notions of individuality or uniqueness which the contemplation of faces can easily encourage, they state that faces are 'not basically individual' (Deleuze and Guattari 1986: 168). They distinguish faciality not only from Sartre's humanist phenomenology but from Lacan's writings on the mirror stage:

> In the literature of the face, Sartre's text on the look and Lacan's on the mirror make the error of appealing to a form of subjectivity or humanity reflected in a phenomenological field or split in a structural field. *The gaze is but secondary in relation to the gazeless eyes, to the black hole of faciality. The mirror is but secondary in relation to the white wall of faciality* (ibid.: 171).

The assertion that faciality is prior to the look and to processes of reflection in general gives it a particular status. The face, according to Deleuze and Guattari, is 'subjacent [*connexe*] to the signifier and the subject'(ibid.: 180), not a site of the production of signifiers, but the condition of possibility of signification, a kind of blank canvas on which new as well as old figurations of the human may be inscribed. Deleuze and Guattari's comments on the 'mask' convey this posthuman conception of the face as skin, surface, detachable layer or blank screen:

> in no case does the mask serve to dissimulate, to hide, even while showing or revealing [. . .] in contrast to primitive societies in which the mask assures/ed the head's belonging to the body, *now* the mask assures the erection, the construction of the face, the facialization of the head and the body: the mask is now the face itself, the abstraction or operation of the face. The inhumanity of the face (ibid.: 181).

The opposition of surface to depth is deconstructed. The mask face of postmodern culture is produced by an 'abstract machine of facialization'. Examples Deleuze and Guattari give of this mechanized production of faces are 'the maternal power operating through the face during nursing; the passional power operating through the face of the loved one [. . .] the political power operating through the face of the leader [. . .] even in mass actions: the power of film operating through the face of the star and the close-up; the power of television' (ibid.: 175). I would suggest that facial cosmetic surgery, rather than being just another domain of sociocultural or political activity to be added to this list, is a practice that reveals the escalating power of the facialization 'machine'. The face in cosmetic surgery has ceased to be a signifier of uniqueness and individuality, and become a detachable, graftable mask, a prosthesis. In their version of this paradigm shift, Deleuze and Guattari go as far as to call the face 'inhuman':

> the face is produced in humanity. But it is produced by a necessity that does not apply to human beings "in general". The face is not animal, but neither is it human in general; there is even something absolutely inhuman about the face [. . .] The inhuman in human beings: that is what the face is from the start (ibid.: 170–1).

The discovery of this inhumanity of the face may even be attributed to cosmetic surgery. The rise of surgery in the 1980s and 1990s has seen it practised on almost every part of the human body, but perhaps what is going on in the surgery boom is what Deleuze and Guattari call the facialization of the entire body ('If the head and its elements are facialized, the entire body also can be facialized', ibid.: 170). Cosmetic surgery's privileging of the face may simply be a continuation of the face's prominence in painted and photographic portraiture, the cinema, and advertising. Postmodern faciality – the inhuman, surface 'mask' face evoked by Deleuze and Guattari – is demonstrated in a number of the large and luridly coloured photographic plates from Orlan's operation 'Omnipresence', and particularly by the image of the surgeon's knife cutting in front of her left ear to lift away her face from the side of her head.

It is undoubtedly significant that the centrality of the face to cosmetic surgery has been repeated in Orlan's work with the practice; although one of the early operations of 'Reincarnation' involved the liposuction of fat from her thighs, all the others have had her face as their object. By making her face the focal point of 'Reincarnation', Orlan has revealed the precariousness of faciality as the seat or site of human qualities and attributes – the literal superficiality of 'humanity' in our postmodern age.

I suggested at the start of this section that the status of the face as signifier of the human is a historically limited phenomenon. It is not difficult to show that the very concept of 'humanity' is bound to the history of modernity. A genealogy of the equation 'face = human' would reveal the multiple biases of the claim to stand in for the universal 'human', which, like any claim to neutral universality, masks and suppresses sexual, racial, geographical and economic differences. Deleuze and Guattari avoid this universalism, and note the masculinism, racism and Eurocentrism inherent in the imagery of faciality: 'The face is not a universal. It is not even that of the white man; it is White Man himself . . . The face is Christ. The face is the typical European [. . .] Racism operates by the determination of degrees of deviance in relation to the White-Man face' (ibid.: 176 and 178). Amongst feminist commentators, Donna Haraway notes the gender bias of viewing the face as a privileged signifier of humanity when she says 'Humanity's face has been the face of man' (Haraway 1992a: 86)

Postmodern culture will not reinstate the White-Man face as an icon except ironically or parodically. The faces and bodies manufactured by the facialization machine of conventional cosmetic surgery reproduce the normative morphologies of race and gender familiar in Western multicultural societies, with one vital difference: the surgical ideal is not the White-Man face but the White-Woman face (Balsamo 1996: 59–63; Kaplan 1997: 258–67). Despite the growth of cosmetic surgery as a practice in all population sectors in the West, including children and the permanently disabled, it is still more prevalent among white people than people of colour, and amongst women rather than men. The popularity among Asian women of upper eyelid blepharoplasty (Balsamo 1996: 62-3), in which an open, Western eyelid is

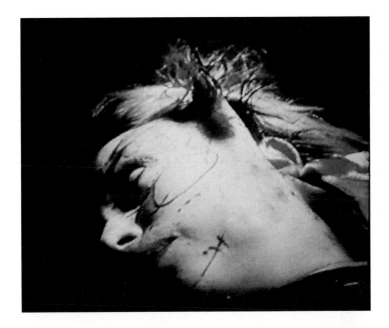

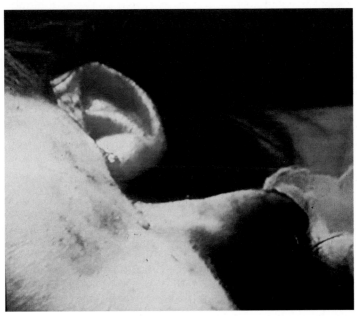

Figure 11. Carnal art 'detachment' ('décollement', of face) during the 7th operation-performance 'Omnipresence', New York, 21 November 1993. Cibachrome in diasec vacuum, 165cm × 110cm. Photo by Vladimir Sichov for SIPA Press.

surgically constructed, is further compelling evidence of the ideologically and economically determined superior beauty of the occidental female face.

In 'Reincarnation', Orlan's face has become the meeting-point of all the discourses on faciality I have traced, art-historical, philosophical, sociological and medical. A surface on which identities have been inscribed and co-exist in tension, it is perhaps the first white woman's face to exhibit the formative influence of all these discourses on the 'human' face of the 1990s. As a morphologically shifting site of conflicting meanings that invites the gazes reserved for monsters, her face is one of the postmodern 'feminist figures of humanity' Donna Haraway calls for to succeed the humanity of modernity. Twentieth-century critiques of subjectivity and representation demand that new images of humanity be very different from the old. As Haraway emphasizes, feminist humanity 'must, somehow, both resist representation, resist literal figuration, and still erupt in powerful new tropes, new figures of speech, new turns of historical possibility'. As feminist figure, Orlan's face has abandoned fixed form and fixed meanings for a future replete with what Haraway calls 'the promises of monsters' (Haraway 1992b: 295).

Frankenstein's Bride

In 1990 Orlan posed for a portrait photograph wearing the wig and make-up of the Bride of Frankenstein, the mate envisaged for Frankenstein's creature in Mary Shelley's famous novel of 1818. With pale face, full lips, a fixed robotic stare and an electric white wave standing out against the piled-high frame of hair, the portrait is a close copy of the image presented by Elsa Lanchester in the 1935 classic film *The Bride of Frankenstein*.[3] In this portrait Orlan was again – as in the 1978 'Documentary Study. The Head of Medusa' – assuming the identity of an instantly recognizable monstrous woman, this time from literary rather than classical mythology.

The Frankenstein myth is more resonant than ever at the turn of the third millenium, when the new reproductive technologies developed in the 1980s and 1990s are raising urgent social and ethical issues about scientific intervention in the creation of life. In vitro fertilization, gene therapy and cloning (particularly human cloning) present advanced societies with dilemmas as to what it is and is not desirable for us to create. The power to create life by non-'natural' means of reproduction, in the laboratory, seemingly

---

3. *The Bride of Frankenstein* was directed by James Whale for Universal Studios in 1935, four years after his *Frankenstein* made Boris Karloff a star (Karloff also takes the leading role in *The Bride of Frankenstein*, considered by many to be a superior film).

Figure 12. Official portrait in Bride of Frankenstein wig, 1990. Cibachrome on aluminium, 110cm × 165cm. Photo by Fabrice Levêque.

makes life draw ever closer to science fiction, and some of its nightmarish visions of the unregulated creation of monstrous and hostile life-forms. In this context, the Frankenstein myth suggests that contemporary society might do well to heed the warnings of its fictional monsters.

To feminist commentators of a postmodern era, however, Frankenstein's monsters are more than warning figures; as a product of the early nineteenth century, they are situated on a border between the human and the non-human characteristic of this stage of modernity, which saw its purification of all non-human elements as part of its scientific and social project. According to Nina Lykke, who draws on the theory of modernity put forward by the French historian of science Bruno Latour, this process of purification was doomed to fail and was, even whilst actively pursued, 'continuously counteracted by an underground proliferation of monsters' (Lykke 1996b: 16). At the end of the twentieth century, with the modern project thoroughly eroded and fragmented, the boundary keeping out monsters no longer holds. Humanity will depend for its survival on new forms and figurations, newly imagined bodies. One of these is the cyborg, or cybernetic organism claimed by Donna Haraway, of which Frankenstein's monsters are an important early fictional manifestation. Following Haraway, Lykke suggests that contemporary feminism may usefully situate itself in the border zone between the human and the non-human, and identify with the monstrous rather than seeking to reject it. Lykke calls upon monsters, goddesses and cyborgs to serve as landmarks in the map of the discursive spaces in which feminism encounters the sciences, natural, social and human.

I shall go on to discuss the links between Orlan's multimedia work and feminist readings of cyborgs in the next section of this chapter. First, bearing in mind the identification it represents, I shall explore in a little more detail the imagery of Orlan's self-portraiture as the Bride of Frankenstein.

Orlan slips on the identity of Frankenstein's bride briefly, just as she is beginning her 1990s work with cosmetic surgery. In Shelley's *Frankenstein* the creation of the Bride is never in fact completed; the monster's desire for a companion and mate compels Victor Frankenstein to undertake the task of preparing her, but Victor, horrified by the ugliness and barbarity of his first 'fiend', is unable to complete his work, and tears the female creature to pieces.[4] The limbs and parts of the monster's bride-to-be are consigned to the bottom

---

4. 'I thought with a sensation of madness on my promise of creating another like to him, and trembling with passion, tore to pieces the thing on which I was engaged. The wretch saw me destroy the creature on whose future existence he depended for happiness, and with a howl of devilish despair and revenge, withdrew' (Shelley 1994: 193).

of the ocean in a basket weighted with stones, with Victor feeling 'almost [. . .] as if I had mangled the flesh of a living human being' (Shelley 1994: 197). The aborted creation of the literary Bride of Frankenstein is, I would suggest, very significant in the history of female cyborgs. Shelley's novel sets out all the questions concerning the legitimate and illegitimate creation of life, and the role of biological science in its creation, and provides some limited description of the appearance of Frankenstein's monster. But it has been left to later, exclusively twentieth-century adapations of her novel, to bring the Bride to life, and to give her a visual identity. Frankenstein is a creature of Romantic Gothic fiction and the beginnings of nineteenth-century modernity, but the Bride belongs to the age of mechanical reproduction, and to the cinema. The imagery of her brief appearances in Whale's film and other cinematic adapations is very suggestive for Orlan's work as a female artist concerned with the impact of science and technology upon human, and especially female human, identity.

Screen adaptations of the Frankenstein story give free rein to the scientific method of the Bride's manufacture, which sometimes differs from that of the original monster. A 1973 film entitled *Frankenstein: The True Story* depicts the Bride as brought to life in a chemical tank. The setting of all dramatizations of Frankenstinian creation, however – most memorably in the two black-and-white Universal films of the 1930s – is the scientific laboratory, with an operating table as its centrepiece, and Victor Frankenstein wearing the robes of a surgeon. In *The Bride of Frankenstein* Elsa Lanchester resembles a mummy, as she is awoken entirely wrapped in bandages. The cinematography of these scenes is enormously dynamic and inventive; while the operating table is raised into the roof to harness natural electrical power (done in *The Bride of Frankenstein* by releasing kites into the storm, a reference to Benjamin Franklin's early experiments with electricity), the feverish scientific work in progress is conveyed by rapid editing and wild diagonal shots of Frankenstein and his assistants. Like the male monster before her, the Bride's first movement is of her right hand, and the scientist's elated cry , 'She's alive! Alive!', exactly echoes his words in the first film.

The first shots of the living Bride pick out her tightly bandaged feminine form, the zomboid raising of her arms, and her eyes' dilated pupils. The action then cuts to the key scene in the film's narrative, in which the Bride rejects her intended mate. Her brief appearance in this scene is the cornerstone of the modern myth she represents; 'half Nefertiti, half ghost with her long white bridal gown, or death robe, or swaddling cloth [. . .] she stands halfway between a zombie and a future punk, outlandishly sexy' (Manguel 1997: 46). Even more significant than the Bride's dress and expression for understanding the image invoked in Orlan's portrait is the concentration of unmistakably sexual power in her head, and in her hair. Elsa Lanchester's Bride is, like a recent performance piece of Orlan's, a 'Woman with Head', her sexuality channelled away from her heavily robed body. The Bride's wig, the main feature of Orlan's portrait, is in fact not strictly a wig, but a combination of prosthetic and human hair.[5] As an artefact, it conveys the Bride's hybrid identity of man-made cyberwoman and monster-with-a-soul, while simultaneously invoking the traditional power of women's hair to symbolize eroticism and animality. Its volume and artificial white waves are a Medusan motif. As Alberto Manguel's analysis of the film shows, there are close intertextual links between the cinematic image of the Bride and Surrealist photography of women by Man Ray and Max Ernst from the 1920s and 1930s, in which flowing, wavy hair is loaded with fetishistic erotic significance. The bride was an important symbolic figure in the art of the interwar period, to which Whale's Frankenstein pictures belong, along with almost all Universal studios' early horror pictures (ibid.: 55–62).

In Whale's film, the spectator's attention is directed by the camera entirely at the Bride's head, which replaces her body as repository of her monstrosity and sexuality. The very few shots of the Bride show a scar running underneath her chin from ear to ear, the mark of the surgical attachment of head to body which features in all scenes of the Bride's manufacture, a less comical, more sinister equivalent to the bolt in the male monster's neck. Other cinematic adapations of the Frankenstein story also feature this emphasis on the head-body division,[6] which can be understood as a physiological equivalent of the metaphysical opposition of body to mind, and the way in which visual representations express and play with the mind-body dichotomy.

---

5. The Bride's hair was 'a complicated construction. Four tiny tight braids were made to stand at the top of Lanchester's head, and on these was anchored a wired horsehair cage about five inches high. Lanchester's own hair was brushed over this structure and the two white hairpieces were applied over the lot' (Manguel 1997: 46).

6. The imagery surrounding the Bride in *Frankenstein: The True Story* (1973, dir. Jack Smight, GB), where the Bride figure is called Prima (the 'first of her species'), is a case in point. In early scenes of this film curiosity has been aroused by Prima's choker, which conceals her incriminating neck-scar, sign of her man-made birth. The death met by Prima/the Bride is the film's dramatic climax. When she rejects the creature at a ball arranged to introduce her to society (an interesting parallel with the earliest cinematic female cyborg, Maria in Fritz Lang's *Metropolis* (1926)), he runs riot in the ballroom. Then, detaching the ribbon choker that conceals where her head has been joined to her body, Frankenstein caresses her neck, and slowly, before horrified spectators scrambling for the exit, pulls off her head. Prima/the Bride is unmade exactly as she was made, with the separation of head and body exposing their joining-together as the core act of her monstrous creation.

The prominence of head over body or frame-filling focus on the head alone, is, it can be argued, particularly important to representations of women and women's representations of themselves, as the head is not a gender-neutral part of the body. Head/Body might well have been one of the binary oppositions governing patriarchal metaphysical thought listed by Hélène Cixous in *The Newly Born Woman* (Cixous and Clément 1986), since whilst the head signifies intelligence, rationality and masculinity, the body is coded as sensible, other to rational thought, and feminine. While female hair almost always connotes sexuality, the head to which it is attached is opposed to sexuality and to the body. To pair the words 'woman' and 'head' works against the grain of patriarchally coded meanings and images. Since the emergence of women's performance art as a full-scale art form in the 1960s, the woman's head has often been chosen by female artists to figure changing attitudes to women and to female corporeality. Orlan's boldest treatment of the subject was her performance for the 1996 ICA festival "Totally Wired", 'Woman with Head', a collaboration with the magician Paul Kieve and the video artist Robin Rambau, where techniques of illusion were used to project her disembodied head alone on a table, reading texts familiar from her operation-performances. Video images of her head from previous works, front, back and inverted, were projected rapidly across the white screen at the back of the performance area.

Although, as I have argued, Orlan's surgical project is interested primarily in the face and in facial features, her head, with its characteristic bobbed hairstyle, exposed brow, and yellow, blue or black quiff, has become an unforgettable part of her image. As in performance and installation video by artists such as Bruce Nauman, her head often fills the frame of projected video images or the screen of TV and video monitors. An exhibition of plates from the Mexico-based work she has undertaken recently consisted of eleven computer-generated images of Orlan's head 'hybridized' with the head-sculptures, bone-structures, decorative prostheses and make-up of Mayan beauties.[7] The shaping of the skull is an important element of this work on the beauty standards of Mexican civilizations. Like Orlan's Bride of Franken-stein picture, these images are all head-and-shoulder portraits which empha-size the head in a dramatic way; Orlan is shown in Picasso-like distortion, crested, petrified, and possessed of either an enlarged bony forehead or a kind of extension to the skull that adds several inches to the height of her head (in Mayan civilization a tall built-up cranium was considered a sign of beauty).

7. 'Self-hybridation', at the Espace d'Art Yvonamor Palix, Rue Keller, Paris, 3/11/98 – 30/1/99.

Figure 13. 'Woman with head', performance at the Institute of Contemporary Arts, London, with magician Paul Kieve, video artist Dean Bramnagann and musician Robin Rambau, April 1996. Black and white photo, 50cm × 60cm, by Gérard Orlow.

I would suggest that there is a double gesture behind Orlan's representation of her head in work since her photo portrait as the Bride of Frankenstein, which works firstly to assert women's capacities of vision and language (capacities associated with the head and traditionally viewed as masculine), and secondly, to drive home that there is no rigid opposition between these attributes and those traditionally viewed as feminine. The head is a part of the body.[8] Representation in a portrait with her amazing hair, bare shoulders and an arm clad in a long black velvet glove (as much vamp as monster) show the Bride of Frankenstein to be a fully sexual creature, but she is also a seeing, equal being, who rejects the role of companion and mate for which the patriarchal world has created her.

8. 'The Head is a Part of the Body' was the title of a performance by the German artist Katharina Sieverding included in François Pluchart's *L'art corporel* (Pluchart 1975).

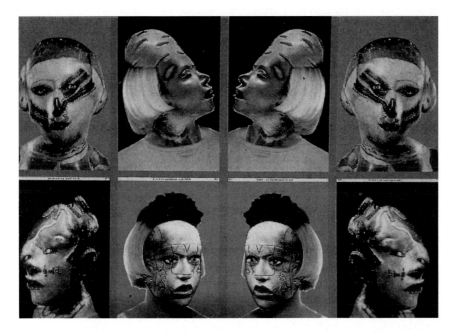

Figure 14. 'Refiguration hybridation', series no. 1, 1997, 110cm × 90cm. Printing and technical assistance by Pierre Zovilé for the Montreal video festival 'Champlibre'. By courtesy of the Yvonamor Palix gallery, Paris.

The brevity of the original cinematic appearance of the Bride of Frankenstein is matched by the single image of her in the gallery of self-portraits as mythological women Orlan has put together since assuming the identity of Saint Orlan in 1971. One image amongst hundreds, its singularity suggests something of its power as a representation of the monstrous feminine. Ugliness, disability and mutilation in the domain of the real are subjects treated more freely in contemporary women's self-portraiture than even twenty years ago, and Orlan's work with mythical monstrous women, the Medusa and the Bride, has developed in parallel with these representations. First imagined by Mary Shelley in 1818 but aborted on the laboratory floor, and granted a visual identity by cinema in the age of the Hollywood studios, it is perhaps in the popular cyborg culture and visual art practice conversant with it that the Bride of Frankenstein has found the era where she is most at home.

Cyborg Orlan: Is the Body Obsolete?

Donna Haraway's 'A Cyborg Manifesto' (Haraway 1991), first published in 1985, established the cyborg, or cybernetic organism, as central to both feminist history and contemporary culture. The history of man-machine hybrids spans the discourses of sociology, medicine, literature and cinema, and can be traced back to well before the twentieth century. Cyborgs are a staple of the science fiction novel from the late nineteenth century on, and present from the very early history of cinema, but it is in late twentieth-century popular culture that they have come into their own – in blockbuster action movies and the merchandise they generate, in the strip cartoons of pulp magazines and on TV, in amusement arcades, video games, and children's toys.

For Haraway and other contemporary commentators, however, the cyborg's status extends well beyond popular culture and media. The cyborg is a political myth intimately bound up with the rise of feminism, and like it, has a major role in shaping the future of humanity. The collective object that is women's experience is, according to Haraway, 'a fiction and a fact', which has been both discovered and constructed by feminism; the social reality of women's oppression is a 'world-changing fiction' (ibid.: 149). Among the continually self-renewing forms of feminist humanity called for by Haraway, the cyborg is privileged because it figures innumerable possible multiple and hybrid identities. Its disrespect of the boundary between fact and fiction conjures prospects of as yet unimagined bodily identities and social formations. Rosi Braidotti stresses that an alliance between cybertheory and recent feminist thinking on the body – what she styles as 'the new interconnection of mothers, monsters and machines' – is positive because it 'has to do with the loss of any essentialized definition of womanhood' (Braidotti 1996c: 94). One of the main emphases of Haraway's manifesto is how scientific and technological discourses, such as those of the new reproductive technologies, are increasingly hegemonic in the constitution of the partial, contradictory and shifting definitions of 'female' that are the legacy of patriarchy and colonialism. Contemporary feminism, like the cyborg, is 'completely without innocence'. Poststructuralist and postmodernist critiques of class consciousness and the concept of community have left cyborg feminists with no illusions about the construction of a common political identity. Against this background, Haraway nonetheless insists that there is now, more than ever, a need for political unity, and that the form the forging of such unity might take is a political myth inspired by socialist feminism (Haraway 1991: 157). The fractured, multivalent identity figured by female cyborgs is the only kind which can still be envisaged in the wake of the 'painful fragmentation' of second-wave feminisms.

The identities that fuel Haraway's 'political-fictional analysis' emerge from the breakdown of the different boundaries that delimit the 'human'. By affirming 'the cyborg appears in myth precisely where the boundary between human and animal is transgressed' (ibid.: 152), Haraway roots her cyborg myth in the past as well as in the present and the future, since this definition of 'cyborg' takes in the satyrs of the Ancient World as well as the many animal-human hybrids of folk tales and fairy stories.

A French folk tale called 'Peau d'âne' (Donkey-Skin), by the seventeenth-century author of *Cinderella* and *Puss-in-Boots*, Charles Perrault, supplied Orlan with material of just this type in an unfinished project that produced some striking images of hybridized femininity, inspired directly by the source-story. 'Peau d'âne' tells how the princess daughter of a widowed king is compelled to flee his kingdom in order to escape her father's incestuous intent to marry her – the only measure that will quell his grief for his dead queen. Once the king has proved the genuineness of his love for Peau d'âne by giving up to her his most precious possession and the secret to the wealth of his kingdom, a donkey that shits gold, flight is the only option left to her. Peau d'âne escapes and successfully remains in hiding for some time thanks to the disguise provided by the donkey-skin. The half-female, half-animal identity she assumes during this period mixes beauty with ugliness, cleanliness with dirt. A number of interpretations of the story have been suggested, but the themes which stand out, and which attracted Orlan to it, are evasion of patriarchal incest (a threat that eventually lifts when the princess finds her own prince and the king marries the fairy who helped her to escape) and the effects of patriarchal desire on female identity. The princess is forced to leave the sociosymbolic space into which she was born and to slip an animal's skin over her own in order to survive, an act that brings out the precariousness and then the ambiguity and hybridity of female identity, as well as the full significance of skin as the purveyor of identity – the surface appearance by which we are seen and recognized (or not). The equivalence of shit and gold in 'Peau d'âne' also speaks volumes, from a psychoanalytic point of view, about the role of sublimation in the constitution of value.

Perrault's tale is also interesting because of the positive connotations it gives to animality, which lacks the base and bestial qualities often associated with it. The princess's bizarre garb causes her no suffering, but simply serves as a protective disguise until the moment when her true beauty is revealed and noble birth identified in a 'Cinderella'-style ceremony at the court of the Prince who has seen her without her donkey-skin, and fallen in love with her. The hybridization of identity in Orlan's set of 'Peau d'âne' pictures anticipates remarkably the fuller and freer treatment of morphed, recomposed female identities displayed in her later self-portraits as Mayan beauties. This ongoing project is working to challenge late twentieth-century conceptions of what female beauty is, and how it is in part determined by viewing expectations, but the images exhibited in 'Self-hybridation' also add up to a striking illustration of Haraway's cyborg myth. Both the 'Peau d'âne' series and the Mayan pictures reveal the fertile potential of division, transformation, mixing and recombination as means of arriving at new female identities, individual and collective.

Orlan's choice of the Bride of Frankenstein for her 1990 self-portrait marked the beginning of her artistic engagement with issues of posthumanity and cyborg identity, but as an experimenter and an activist she was involved in these areas considerably earlier. Throughout the 1980s her work engaged in new media-related projects which brought it into the sphere of technologies of the body. She was one of the first French artists to start to exploit the potential of the new digital media for contemporary art practice, and in 1984 co-founded an on-line arts review magazine, Art-Accès, to promote and broadcast new media-related work. This was available over the Minitel, a state-run information and communications network accessible in France via France Télécom – a kind of precursor to the Internet. In 1986 Art-Accès was used as the medium in her participation in a piece of work by Daniel Buren, 'Mouvements-recouvrements', along with the computer networking medium Videotex. The Centre Georges Pompidou organized the event 'Videotex and Creation' in 1987, and a workshop was devoted to the medium at Louvain (Belgium) in 1989, both events to which Orlan contributed. She was also represented in the major French exhibition of the mid-1980s to investigate immateriality, Jean-François Lyotard's 'Les Immatériaux' at the Centre Georges Pompidou, in 1985,[9] where the dominant issues raised were those of the absent body, synthetic body parts, dematerialization and invisibility.

Installations at the numerous video festivals in which Orlan participated in the 1980s presented fragments of a mediatized body – in the white and black virgins series often a single breast – that linked this fragmentation to its encoding into electronic signals (electronic inscription further fetishised an already fetishistically presented figure). In related performance work where Orlan was present in person, such as 'Saint Orlan and the Elders', video screens of body images were placed in front of or around her, again emphasizing her body's mediatization. Two pieces of work that threw into sharp relief Saint Orlan's insertion of Catholic iconography into the computer

9. Also at 'Les transinteractifs', MacLuhan Science Center, Toronto, 1989.

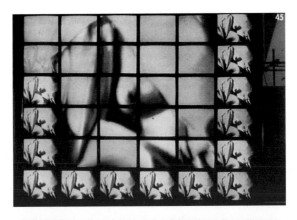

Figure 15. Multi-screen mises en scène nos. 1, 8 & 3, from the videos 'Saint Orlan
and the Elders' and 'Mise en scène for a grand Fiat', shown at the
Toulouse festival of new technologies 1986. Colour photos mounted on
aluminium, 3 × 110cm × 165cm.

age, both shown in 1989, were 'The Madonna on the Minitel' ('La madone au minitel') at the Palais de Tokyo, and the punningly entitled 'Femmes cathodiques', at the International Video Festival Simone de Beauvoir, Paris.[10]

Orlan's works with electronic and digital media conform to the first of the two main types of cyborg identity, according to which information about the body is encoded into a cybernetic system. An interface between body and computer upsets the dualism of organism and machine by opening up a channel through which information may pass between them. Digitally encoded information traverses the conventional bodily limit of the skin, and extends 'the body' to wherever the information is retrieved. The most striking example to date of such a cybernetic body, outside science fiction, has been the entire human body digitally encoded and placed on the Internet in 1994, where it supplies medical scientists with minute biological knowledge at the touch of a button, and, through the presentation of images, serves as a manipulable virtual mannequin for surgical procedure.[11] (Remote 'tele'-surgery carried out via computer-transmitted signals to mechanically operated instruments is one medical advance recently enabled by digital encoding of the body.) Stelarc, the Australian body artist who performs with a robotic 'third arm', is undoubtedly the performer who has most fully investigated the permeability of boundaries between the physical and the virtual body. In recent performances Stelarc has connected his body up to the Internet, in order to give live demonstrations of the construction and mediatization of the material body by communications technologies.

Orlan's self-portrait as the Bride of Frankenstein marked the start of an engagement with the second type of cyborg body, the coupling between a human being and an electronic or mechanical apparatus. As with the digitalization of the body, the human-machine distinction breaks down, and the boundary between the 'natural' and the 'technological' body is redrawn.[12] Scientific and medical advances of the last twenty years, many of them in surgery, have blurred the boundaries between human bodies and the androids or 'replicants' familiar from science fiction literature and cinema. Practices

10. Exhibitions and festivals of art and technology in which Orlan has participated more recently include the 1995 Lyon biennial of art and new technology, a new technologies festival at the University of Warwick (UK) in 1995, the 1996 ICA 'Totally wired' series, Montreal's 'Champ libre' in 1997 (3rd international manifestation of video and electronic art), and the Fondation Miro's 'corps et technologie' event in Barcelona in 1997.

11. The body was that of executed killer Joseph Paul Jernigan, a 39-year old Texan who had donated his body to medicine. After his execution his body was frozen in gelatin and sliced into 1,870 sections, each of which was photographed to create a 3-D image. Annie Griffin, 'We can rebuild him', article on Stelarc, *Guardian* 4 May 1996, p. 26.

12. See Anne Balsamo, *Technologies of the Gendered Body*, Introduction p.11 and Chapter 1.

that form cyborg bodies and that have been becoming common in the 1990s are transplants of animal organs to human beings, the laboratory growth of skin to be used in surgical grafting, and the increasing use by medicine of prostheses of all kinds. Orlan's forehead implants resemble alien antennae, and give her an other-worldly appearance that directly invoke a cyborg identity. At the beginning of her presentations of surgical operation-performances she sometimes quips that she will speak French rather than the audience's language, as she has forgotten her multilingual translation neurotransmitters, which may be imagined embedded in the antennae-like bumps above her eyebrows. One of the two future operations she still speaks of planning is an unspecific enhancement of her faculties that suggests neurosurgery and/or a programmed modification of her personality. And although the morphed images of her surgically 'ideal' face have already drawn extensively on the idea of virtual identity, she has plans to go one stage further; one of the works shown in the touring exhibition starting at the Carrillo Gil Museum in Mexico early in 1999 was an interactive video installation of a talking clone of herself. This will be linked to her investigations of the beauty standards of Mexican civilizations through the inscription of Aztec riddles upon the clone's body: the clone is a technological hybrid of ancient and postmodern.

The operations of 'The Reincarnation of Saint Orlan' have not (so far) involved the implantation of mechanically or electronically operated components in Orlan's body, or the modification of genetic material. Prosthetics and genetic therapy are at the cutting edge of contemporary biotechnology, but can nonetheless be seen as forming a continuum with the techniques of surgical body modification and digital resdesign employed in 'Reincarnation'. To describe this less extreme set of practices, which nonetheless still qualify as cyborg phenomena, Rachel Armstrong coins the term 'Euphenics', which she explains as follows:

> With the advances of modern biotechnology, it is not necessary to wait for the arrival of genetic mutation to upgrade the properties of the human subject. The mechanisms of human adaptation have changed. These non-genetic measures are Euphenic methods. The term is derived from the phenotype of an organism which refers to its visible appearance or function. Euphenics may be considered to affect the function and development of the individual external to the inherent adaptive genetic mechanisms (Armstrong 1995: 56)

According to Armstrong, Euphenics is already routine in clinical practice, relied upon by people regarded as healthy and normal. Its range of treatments and techniques is reputable, and is already being drawn upon by most people in their lifetimes. Examples Armstrong cites include now standard medical treatments such as antibiotics (which augment the immune system), and the contraceptive pill (which controls the cycle of hormones). It is the path technological human evolution is following, regardless of individual or collective choice. For Armstrong, the importance of Orlan's 1990s work has been to make this stage of bodily human evolution visible to a wide public. Since the field of Euphenics is appearance, it is obvious territory for contemporary body art. The complexification of medicine that Euphenics designates is making the distinction between the 'natural' and the technologically and discursively constructed body impossible to draw. Before long, we will all be cyborgs – if we aren't already.

Orlan's 1980s and 1990s work can therefore be seen to draw on both types of cyborg body outlined by commentators on the field – the digitally encoded, virtual body, and the human-machine coupling made possible by the ever-advancing sophistication of contemporary surgery. However, neither of these models of bodily construction quite matches a strain in her discourse of self-transformation which seeks to eclipse the material body altogether.

> Like the Australian artist Stelarc, I think that the body is obsolete. It is no longer adequate for the current situation. We mutate at the rate of cockroaches, but we are cockroaches whose memories are in computers, who pilot planes and drive cars that we have conceived, although our bodies are not designed for these speeds. We are on the threshold of a world for which we are neither mentally nor physically ready (Orlan 1996: 91).

The 'world' to which Orlan refers here could be the interior space of virtual reality programs, the applications of which in industry, advertising, communications and entertainment are already extensive. In the virtual worlds of cyberspace, the physical body is entirely absent, subjective agency having passed to an imaginary gender-free, race-free site which corresponds to no location in the material world. As Anne Balsamo points out in a critique of the notion of the virtual body, abandoning the problematic of the constructed body implicates virtual reality technologies in the reproduction of the most traditional cultural narrative of all – transcendence, whereby 'the physical body and its social meanings can be technologically neutralized' (Balsamo 1996: 128). VR applications offer an alluring but escapist dream, whose replication of real-world spaces does nothing to encourage reflection on the functioning of visual representation. Not only do virtual reality programs have no performative capacity to create 'disembodied citizens' that correspond to the worlds it offers its users, they have nothing to teach us about the bodies in which our subjectivities are situated while we access them. Most crucial of all for feminists, the disembodied perspective assumed by VR technology indisputably involves a gender bias against the new understandings of embodiment made possible by feminist research (Balsamo 1996: 123).

Alternatively and more probably, Orlan's mention of a future in which the body is obsolete may refer to a type of evolution in which the human body can no longer keep pace with machine and computer technology. According to this vision evolution is not tending towards an expanded definition of 'human', materially realized in a proliferation of hybridized bodies. Instead, where it is headed, whether by technological accident or design, is towards the development of artificial intelligences that do not require to be located in material bodies. Intelligence is the software, the body just hardware for which a range of durable non-humanoid containers can be substituted. The enormous growth of communications technologies in the closing years of the twentieth century has led some technology writers to speculate that the decisive shift towards artificial forms of intelligence has already taken place, and that in the near future computers will be able to simulate not only the memory capacity but the creative intelligence of the human mind.

Discussing this aspect of Orlan's work, Sandy Stone expresses the view that the obsolescence of the human body is an assumption linked to the final stages of late capitalism, but suggests the assumption is linked to a deeper one, according to which the link between body and self, an alternative and inadequate term for which would be 'intellect', is in fact 'infinitely plastic and malleable'. It is extremely improbable, in Stone's opinion, that a stage of evolution will be reached in which the body has been eclipsed altogether. What current writing about this possibility bears witness to is a profound symbolic shift in human thinking about the relationships of body, mind, self and thought, from which intellectual capacity is beginning to emerge strengthened and more self-aware (Stone 1996: 49).

Striking though it is, Orlan's suggestion that she is headed towards disembodied realms of intelligence seems directly at odds with other aspects of the 'Reincarnation' project. Her speculation about the obsolescence of the body sets up a contradiction in her autobiographical statements which can perhaps only be explained if we accept her desire for the future, but do not see her as wholly embracing the technological field – she has insisted on occasion that she is not an artist 'of the new technologies'.[13] Orlan does not have a body, she is one. And however great the modifications effected in the course of her reincarnation, she will still be one. The permanency of the self-

13. At the event 'Digital Landscapes of the Mind' at the Cochrane Theatre, Central St Martin's College of Art & Design, London, 5 November 1997.

transformation she is carrying out is perhaps the most disturbing aspect of her project; although she intends, plans and choreographs her surgical performances, the different body she is left with after each operation is not something she can totally control. Although it is at the core of her work, the art object par excellence, Orlan's body in some sense also escapes the very artistic process it makes possible. And without bodily appearance, the vital art-historical side of the project is completely lost. The notion that the material body will be superseded by disembodied forms of intelligence undermines the materialist feminist reading of 'Reincarnation' she has encouraged by affirming that the project can be seen as an acting-out of all the social and cultural pressures Western capitalist societies place upon the female body (Orlan 1996: 35). If the material body is destined for the rubbish-heap of history, why bother to redesign it at all? It seems much wiser and more appropriate not to endorse Orlan's speculation about the obsolescence of the human body, but to consider cyborg as one of the many identities she employs in her continuous process of discursive identity construction. It is an identity – or set of identities – she has employed to powerful effect in 'Reincarnation' and more recent work of the 1990s, and a rich source of images and ideas she is likely to continue to draw on in the twenty-first century.

Between the Acts: Postmodern Performance Art, Cosmetic Surgery, and the Feminist Performative Reconstruction of Female Subjectivity

From Presence to Omnipresence: Media, Technology and Performance Art

In my discussions of Orlan's art practice in previous chapters, I have often described her works and performances as postmodern, without discussing further the contested history of this term. For many people, 'postmodern(ist)' and 'postmodernism' are words that have acquired so many multiple and conflicting meanings that they have become overinflated and lost their currency. In one sense too, 'postmodern' has simply turned into a conventional way of historicizing the contemporary, and to tag Orlan with its label is just to make the obvious observation that she is an artist of her age, using up-to-the-minute electronic media. It is clear, however, that Orlan's work possesses many of the characteristics of art and culture agreed on as 'postmodern' by the majority of postmodernism's commentators; one striking example is the recombination and permutation of images from one work to the next, particularly in evidence in 'Reincarnation'. In the first part of this final chapter, then, I would like to consider Orlan's technological, multimedia work in the context of debates about postmodern performance. The incorporation of media technology into body and performance art of the 1980s and 1990s has been a key factor in distinguishing contemporary practice of these art forms from the work of the genres' pioneers in the 1950s and 1960s. Central to discussion of technological performance art has been the concept of presence, and in considering what Orlan's work may contribute to debates about postmodern performance, and what these debates suggest about the (post)modernity of her art practice, I shall discuss in particular which, if any, concept of presence is most helpful in defining what we mean by 'postmodern' performance.

As Marvin Carlson observes in his recent critical introduction to performance, the issue of its postmodernity has not really been addressed by one specific theorist in the way that Charles Jencks has written about postmodern architecture, and Sally Banes about postmodernism in dance (Carlson 1996: 132). In his discussion of performance and the postmodern, Carlson assesses the work of theorists of performance in relation to the two most influential critics of modernism in art, Clement Greenberg and Michael Fried. It was Greenberg's essay 'Recentness of Sculpture' that introduced the concept of presence to the analysis of modern art, and when discussing this essay, Fried concluded that the kind of presence Greenberg attributed to the art work was in fact inimical to the modernist art project. Carlson summarizes:

> Such presence, Fried remarks, might in fact be called a kind of "stage" presence, and as such is antithetical to the essential minimalist project, which rejects the situation or the interaction with a viewer to be wholly manifest within itself. Similarly, Fried denies any effect of duration in the art experience, presence being available in the perceptual instant and duration of experience being "paradigmatically theatrical" (Carlson 1996: 125).

Fried's summary pronouncement on modernist art was 'The success, even the survival, of the arts has come increasingly to depend on their ability to defeat theatre' (ibid.: 126).

In my analyses of Orlan's performances, I have argued that the situation of the art work and its interaction with the viewer – through the dynamics of viewing relations – are central. As far as the effect of duration of experience is concerned, I agree with the account of performance art given in a recent book by Gérard Genette, where Genette considers the main ways in which this art form may be characterized in relation to duration (*durée*). He proposes that the duration possessed by the objects of performance art is, rather than a 'duration of persistence' (*durée de persistance*), a duration of process (*durée de procès*). 'It is obvious that in this sense performance works are "temporal" objects, whose duration of process participates in their specific identity, objects that can only be experienced in this duration of process' (Genette 1994: 73).[1]

---

1. 'C'est évidemment en ce sens que les oeuvres de performance sont des objets "temporels", dont la durée de procès participe à l'identité spécifique, des objets qu'on ne peut éprouver que dans cette durée de procès.'

Orlan's body art seems unequivocally to illustrate Genette's notion of a 'duration of process'; her body disrupts the very definition of the stable art 'object', but in so far as it is an object, it is a fully temporalized one, displaying 'process' rather than 'persistence'.

So in my readings of Orlan's performances, Michael Fried's interpretation of Clement Greenberg's theory of presence – the notion that the art work allows duration of experience, makes demands to be taken into account by the viewer, and possesses a kind of presence that is stagey and theatrical – certainly applies to Orlan's work. In this respect she does not conform at all to Fried's definition of modernism (Greenbergian presence is what the modernist art work must avoid at all costs), but is much more aptly characterized as postmodern. This does not mean, however, that I want to argue that Orlan's work shares none of the characteristics of the modernist project. One theorist central to modernist art practice with whom she has repeatedly been linked is Antonin Artaud, and by illustrating her links to the aesthetics of Artaud's Theatre of Cruelty, I shall try to show how Orlan makes visible a continuum between modernist and postmodernist performance. As far as the type of presence characteristic of Orlan's performances is concerned, I shall also suggest that Walter Benjamin's concept of the 'aura' of the work of art put forward in his seminal essay 'The Work of Art in the Age of Mechanical Reproduction', where 'aura' names what is destroyed by the ever-increasing mechanical reproducibility of (post)modernist culture, has continuing relevance to Orlan's body art.

In performance art up to and including the 1960s and 1970s generation of body artists, the dominant kind of presence was the 'live', physical presence of the performer/performer's body. The immediacy to the audience of this type of presence may be characterized as phenomenological, in so far as it drew attention to the simple activity of being there (Carlson 1996: 127). This kind of phenomenological presence became central to performance's place in modernist art, despite Fried's warnings. For the early practitioners of body art such as Piero Manzoni, Gina Pane, Vito Acconci and Rudolf Schwarzkogler, the body was a new and authentic medium untapped by processes of representation, and it was by identifying with the body (usually their own bodies) as site of the art work that these artists sought to construct their performances. In so far as the presentation or 'making-present' of their bodies as a kind of site of truth seemed possible to them, this first generation of body artists conformed to a thoroughly modernist aesthetic of performance, in which 'presence' was a value to be pursued and embraced.

As Robert Fleck explains in an essay for the catalogue to the huge retrospective exhibition of performance art that took place at the Centre

Georges Pompidou in Paris in 1995, 'Hors Limites: l'art et la vie 1952–1994', the main difference between the first and the contemporary generations of body artists lies in their differing attitudes towards the possibility of an 'authentic' bodily presence. The early 1990s had already seen a number of exhibitions – Jeffrey Deitch's 'Post Human', Paul Schimmel's 'Helter Skelter' at the Los Angeles Museum of Contemporary Art, and Documenta 9 in Kassel (the most-visited show of contemporary art ever with 600,000 entries) in which this new conception of the body was becoming apparent (Fleck 1994: 311–12). Although a revival of body art and of the spirit of 1950s and 1960s happenings was unquestionably underway by 1992, the new generation of body artists was approaching the body with none of the innocence of their 1960s predecessors. As Fleck puts it,

> The body had been discovered as a separate medium in the plastic arts by the happening, Fluxus, body art and performance in the 1960s. But this new body art of the 1990s no longer reacted in a "postmodern" way, with citations and simulations, to the "historic" body art of the decade 1960–1970 [. . .]. Instead, performance, happening and body art were used in a radically new way and transformed into such original generic forms that the direct influence of the decade 1960–1970 was scarcely noticeable (Fleck 1994: 312–13).

A similar point is made in different terms by Jeff Rian in an important 1993 article for the journal *Flash Art*, 'What's All This Body Art?'[2] Taking Kiki Smith, Charles Ray, Robert Gober, Cindy Sherman, Matthew Barney and Sue Williams as his examples, Rian affirms that in 1990s body art, technology has usurped nature. The body can no longer be celebrated as an unmediated site of identification for the artist, or as an authentic pre-representational physical presence that can be affirmed *as* present in performance. Works by Kiki Smith, Cindy Sherman and Charles Ray show a fascination not with a pre-technological 'natural' body, but with mannequins and automata, as often dismembered as they are unified into a whole human form (Rian 1993: 52). Works by other contemporary body artists employ film, video and a wide variety of other electronic media. The assumption that performance art is all about or is aiming to present the 'live' physical body has been completely transformed by its exploitation of media technology that began in the late 1970s and 1980s, a period described in Roselee Goldberg's updated history of twentieth-century performance as the time of 'the media generation'.[3]

2. 'What's All This Body Art?', *Flash Art* Vol. XXVI, No. 168 (Jan/Feb 1993), 50–3.

3. Goldberg's account of the mediatization of performance from the late 1970s on emphasizes the popularization and commercialization of performance that came about as a result of its

Orlan's career as a performance artist spans both the first and contemporary generations of body artists. The immediate, authentic physical presence of the body espoused in the art of the 1960s and 1970s is obviously a value in her early actions, which did not use any electronic media; her very early 'slowed-down walks' in the street, her measurings of public spaces with her body, and her early appearances as Saint Orlan demonstrate this type of bodily presence. The arrival of poststructuralist theory in the 1970s, and in particular of Derridean deconstruction, posed a head-on challenge to the aesthetics of presence, and simultaneously to this phenomenological approach to performance. But as Carlson succinctly summarizes,

> as this modernist view of performance was fading, it was gradually replaced by a postmodernist view of performance, one that did not give up the vocabulary of "presence" and "absence", or of "theatre" and "performance", but that treated these terms and their relationships in a radically different way (Carlson 1996: 134).

One of the main critics to take on the task of redefining presence in a way which might be useful to less straightforwardly 'live', more mediatized performance was Chantal Pontbriand, who in 1982 put the crucial question of how the presence characteristic of performance is related to the concept of presence central to philosophical enquiry:

> Is [. . .] the presence evinced by contemporary art when there is a meeting between the performer and his public, when there is a performance situation [. . .] – is that presence similar to the one which concerns classical philosophy? (Pontbriand 1982: 155)

Pontbriand's own response to this question is that if continuity is conceded between the presence of classical philosophy and the presence of performance (in a 'performance situation', a meeting between the performer and his public), this is a retrograde step and an indication of decadence. Pontbriand infers very strongly that it would be 'more interesting and plausible' to conceive of a notion of 'neo-presence' that has broken ties with the presence of philosophy, or is 'simply different' from it (ibid.). This step in her argument exactly resembles the move made by those theorists of postmodernism who are unwilling to concede any continuity between modernist and postmodernist

---

being discovered and accepted by the media world. This is probably truer of mainstream US performers like Laurie Anderson than of European practitioners such as Orlan, still very much part of a visual arts avant-garde, but the nature and timing of the mediatization of performance is comparable throughout the Western world.

art or culture, the 'postmodernists of reaction' who insist on a clean break at the inception – logical or historical – of postmodernity. Pontbriand goes on to make it explicit that her aim is indeed 'to draw a distinction between classical presence and post-modern presence' (ibid.).

The term 'Omnipresence' used by Orlan as the title of her seventh operation-performance suggests something very like Pontbriand's postmodern presence. 'Omnipresence' was relayed by live video and satellite link-ups to art galleries and media centres across the world, and employed numerous other forms of media technology, such as the fax Orlan used to answer questions from her audience. Along with the highly technological Internet-based performances of Stelarc and a small number of other performers in the 1990s, the operation marked a kind of culmination of performance art's exploitation of electronic media that began in the 1970s and 1980s. In 'Omnipresence', there was no longer any 'live' body on show to the audience, phenomenologically speaking (there was strictly speaking no audience in the operating theatre, unless one counts Orlan herself and her team of medical and media personnel). The body had become digitally saturated, thoroughly and completely mediatized by the images and electronic signals transmitting the surgery to the world beyond the operating theatre. Orlan's 'omnipresence' was achieved via media technology, and was as such a prime example of postmodern media culture, in which physical reality has given way entirely to mediatized reality, and referents are subsumed in the continuous circulation of signs.

However, although Orlan's mediatized surgical performances seem to demonstrate exactly the definition of 'neo-presence' or postmodern presence given by Chantal Pontbriand, questions remain as to whether they really have no ties at all to the modernist aesthetic of performance derived from the presence theorized by classical philosophy, and exemplified in earlier performance art. Early performance had much in common with the theories of theatre put forward by Antonin Artaud in his 1930s manifesto *The Theatre and Its Double*, which represented a violent reaction against theatrical tradition. The type of theatre Artaud set out in *The Theatre and Its Double* rejected the traditional pre-eminence of language, dialogue, character and narrative, and sought to substitute for them a sort of theatre of the body which employed gesture, space, sound and colour. As Marvin Carlson states, 'Early performance, such as body art [. . .] shared certain of Artaud's concerns, and came closer than most subsequent performance to addressing them. Such performance sought what might be characterized as a physical rather than a psychic essentialism' (Carlson 1996: 126). In their pursuit of an artistic essentialism, Artaud's theories of theatre had much in common with Fried's notion of minimalist modernism: 'Artaud too sought an art complete within itself, in which both the passage of time and the split between the observer and observed ceased to exist' (ibid.).

As I have argued above, it seems senseless to claim that Orlan's 1990s surgical performances aspire to the physical essentialism that would unambiguously characterize them as modernist. Her career is a particularly good illustration of the evolution of performance art from its 1960s essentialist modernism to its thoroughly postmodern 1990s mediatization. But it would also be shortsighted to overlook the striking resonances that exist between her theatre of the body and the ideas put forward by Artaud in *The Theatre and Its Double*. Like Artaud, Orlan is preoccupied by space, gesture, colour, sound and music. 'Reincarnation' seems in many ways to have achieved the physical 'language' Artaud dreamt of restoring to Western theatre. Orlan is of course not actually working in the genre/medium of theatre, and does not have to contend with or defy the Western theatrical tradition of character, dialogue and weighty psychological narrative, but she has nonetheless given a particularly dramatic display of the notion of 'cruelty' – a cruelty of spectacle, not violence – developed by Artaud in his manifestos on theatre. And in her operation-performances, all aspects of the performer's and the spectator's bodies and senses are called upon and put into play.

In 1936 a different but more reasoned and theoretical account than Artaud's of the relationship of art and technological media to presence was put forward by Walter Benjamin in 'The Work of Art in the Age of Mechanical Reproduction'. Chantal Pontbriand gives a useful summary of Benjamin's argument about the aura of the work of art:

In his famous essay 'The Work of Art in the Age of Mechanical Reproduction', Walter Benjamin has dealt at length with presence in relation to the work of art, the aura which he describes as 'the unique phenomenon of a distance, however close it may be' (Benjamin 1936: 243). Mechanical reproducibility, in Benjamin's view deriving from 'the desire of the contemporary masses to bring things "closer" spatially and humanly . . .' (Benjamin 1936: 225), has heralded the disappearance of this aura.[. . .] With performance, it is actuality which is all-important, therefore situation, presentation. Elsewhere in his essay, Benjamin comes around indirectly to this idea of presentation: he explains that exhibition value has replaced cult value. That is to say, cult value, dependent on the uniqueness of the work, finds itself considerably lessened by the advent of reproducibility which makes it possible to multiply the work, to make it accessible, to bring it close. (Pontbriand 1982: 155–6)

While not wanting to make facile claims about Orlan's 'aura' as a performer, there does seem to be a compelling argument that her surgical performance project possesses a kind of 'cult value', in an age when examples of cult value are hard to come by, and alongside the undoubted exhibition value of the frequently reproduced (if not mass-produced) images of her body in the operating theatre. Orlan herself has written about the odd kind of example 'Reincarnation' has set a generation of visual and body artists,[4] and on a number of occasions when I have discussed her surgical work with people, a kind of puzzlement and wonder has descended on the conversation as a mutual effort is made to describe what we (commentators all too aware of how to be unfashionable in a postmodernist climate) are hesitant to term the 'originality' or 'uniqueness' of the idea behind 'Reincarnation'. One way to pinpoint this apparent cult value of Orlan's surgical project is by asking if there would now, post-1990, be any point in any other performance artist undertaking to work with cosmetic surgery in a comparable way?

If there is residual cult value amidst Orlan's exhibition value, lingering modernism in her postmodernism, then tracing her evolution from modernist to postmodernist ways of 'presenting' the body (which in postmodern guise, arguably, results in no kind of 'presence' at all) nonetheless proves very interesting; her use of sophisticated media technology in the 1990s has advanced on the variety of multimedia work she did as Saint Orlan in the 1980s. The advent and increasing prominence of video in her 1980s exhibitions and installations shows Orlan restoring or re-presenting images of her 'lost' live body, not out of nostalgia for its presence (it was often still present alongside the video monitors), but in an exploration of the medium's representational potential.[5] Anna Price compares Orlan's use of video to the work of Nam June Paik, Bill Viola, Richard Serra, Rebecca Horn and Gary Hill, all of whom 'have sought to explore and counteract alienations between the body and technology through video' (Price 1995: 50). As Jeff Rian and Robert Fleck argue in their surveys of body art of the 1980s and early 1990s, the work of most performers of this period shows them coming to terms with the postmodern loss of truth, authenticity and presence, without necessarily resorting to the cliché of producing multiple replicated and

---

4. 'My work has touched a nerve [. . .] In my wake, a lot of artists who are now well known (Matthew Barney, Damien Hirst, Simon Costin, Serge Comte, Valérie Granger, Jack (sic) and Dinos Chapman, Franco B., Made in Eric . . .) and a lot of other young artists who I meet in art schools and who haven't yet been spotted, have started to delve into the imagery of surgery and the mutant body' (Orlan 1998: 99).

5. It could of course be argued that there is nostalgia for the present physical body in Orlan's media works, even that the penetration and evacuation of the flesh by surgical instruments and the camera's eye during her operations is seeking to restore an elusive lost presence. But in this case the presence in question could not be of the (unified) physical performing body, but would be a kind of presence of the flesh, arguably impossible to capture and not really ever present as such (in the terms of classical philosophy).

simulated images of the lost body. The sheer quantity of mediatized self-images characterizing much of Orlan's 1980s work certainly reveals anxiety about the shift from a live performing body to an electronically transmitted one, but the images are always carefully placed and composed, not gratuitously amassed. To quote a very hackneyed dictum of postmodernism, in Orlan's work of the 1980s and 1990s, the medium often is the message. The recycling of self-images between and across media she began to practise intensively in the 1980s shows her undertaking the mediatization of her body required of her generation of artists by the late twentieth-century proliferation of media technology. At the same time, Orlan's 1980s and 1990s performances maintain strong links with earlier generations of body artists through their Artaudian emphasis on spectacle and mise en scène, and their suggestion of an originality or 'uniqueness' resistant to total mechanical reproducibility or electronic mediatization. In at least these ways, Orlan's performance art demonstrates a continuum between modernist and postmodernist performance, and the instability – and perhaps impossibility – of a hard-and-fast, rigid distinction between modernist and postmodernist art and culture.

Between the Acts: Time and (non-)Teleology in 'The Reincarnation of Saint Orlan'

The exhibition of photographic plates from Orlan's 1993 operation 'Omnipresence' that toured the UK from Newcastle to Edinburgh and London in 1996/7 was entitled 'Between Two'. The title drew attention not to the fixity of identity but to what is between the shifting visual identities assumed by (and conferred upon) Orlan in 'Reincarnation'. Between-ness, or the notion of the interval, has been fundamental to the project, not only to its exploration of visual identity-in-process – the conventionally unrepresented post-operative phase of surgery – but to the project's very structure, which will have comprised about ten operations spread out over a number of years, with intervals of varying lengths between them. (In the intervals between operations, precedence is taken by the exhibition and utilization of the artworks they have generated.) The questions of between-ness (the interval), process and finitude are central to twentieth-century debates about performance; Marvin Carlson quotes approvingly from one of the main early histories of performance art,[6] as follows, 'The history of performance art in the twentieth century is the history of a permissive, open-ended medium with endless

6. Roselee Goldberg's *Performance Art: From Futurism to the Present* (Thames and Hudson, 1988) was first published as *Performance: Live Art 1909 to the Present* in 1979.

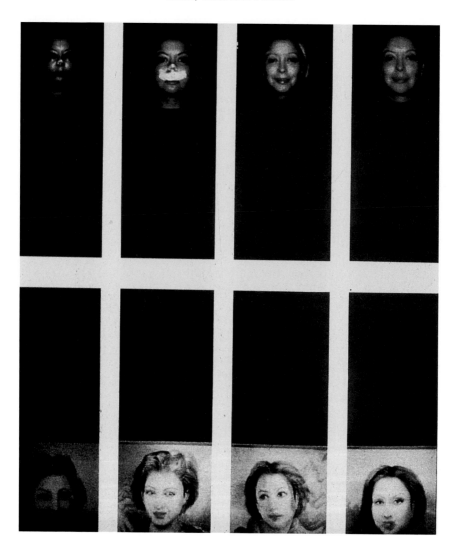

Figure 16a. Forty-one metal diptyches and eighty-two colour photos. Done on silicon screen, with the image produced by Jacques Fretty's morphing programme on silicon material from the Brouillard Précis workshops in Marseilles. Photos of Orlan by Raphaël Cuir, one photo per day obtained for forty-one days after the 7th operation-performance 'Omnipresence', carried out on 21 November 1993 by Marjorie Cramer, costume by Lan Vu, performance transmitted by satellite to the Centre Georges Pompidou, the Banff Multimedia Centre, the McLuhan Centre in Toronto, and the Sandra Gering Gallery in New York. Each diptych 30cm × 150cm, 15m long in total. Picture is by Georges Meguerditchian of the installation at the Centre Georges Pompidou.

Figure 16b. Forty-one metal diptyches and eighty-two colour photos. Done on silicon screen, with the image produced by Jacques Fretty's morphing programme on silicon material from the Brouillard Précis workshops in Marseilles. Photos of Orlan by Raphaël Cuir, one photo per day obtained for forty-one days after the 7th operation-performance 'Omnipresence', carried out on 21 November 1993 by Marjorie Cramer, costume by Lan Vu, performance transmitted by satellite to the Centre Georges Pompidou, the Banff Multimedia Centre, the McLuhan Centre in Toronto, and the Sandra Gering Gallery in New York. Each diptych 30cm × 150cm, 15m long in total. Picture is by Georges Meguerditchian of the installation at the Centre Georges Pompidou.

variables, executed by artists impatient with the limitations of more established art forms' (Carlson 1996: 79).

A summary of the timing of the operations of 'Reincarnation' opens up the questions of temporality raised by Orlan's surgical project. After a performance initiating the work in Newcastle on 30 May 1990, the first, second and third and fourth operations all took place in Paris the same year, the first two at the end of July, the third in September, and the fourth in December. The fifth operation also took place in Paris, on 6 July 1991. An interval of nineteen months elapsed before the 1993 series that comprised the sixth, seventh, eighth and ninth operations. Apart from the operation entitled 'Sacrifice' in Liège, Belgium in February 1993, this group, which included 'Omnipresence', all took place in New York with surgeon Dr Marjorie Cramer. (The eighth and ninth operations followed within a month of 'Omnipresence', in December 1993.) Considered from the perspective of the exposure Orlan has had since 1993, and the currency attributed to 'Reincarnation', the three-and-a-half year period into which all her operation-performances to date have fitted seems short, and the intervals between some of the performances – weeks in two cases – strikingly short. A little-publicized fact is that the necessity for corrective surgery has dictated the timing of some of the operations.

What is now most noticeable when speaking or writing about 'Reincarnation' in the present tense is the length of time that has elapsed since the ninth operation in 1993. In much of the academic and journalistic ink spilled over the project during its active three-and-a-half year phase and the years immediately following, the speculative finale of the project was the operation Orlan would have in Japan to build her nose up into a gigantic elongated feature starting in the centre of her forehead. It now seems unlikely that this concluding operation will ever take place, and I have argued in Chapter 3 for the significance of this change of heart and change of direction. When speaking to me in August 1998 about her future plans for surgery, and in an article published at around the same time, Orlan mentioned just two further operations she may have, and then only if she has all the medical, artistic and financial guarantees that will enable her to work in optimum conditions. One would be a simple 'poetic' surgery consisting of the making of an incision in Orlan's arm from underneath her armpit down towards her elbow, to illustrate the importance of the action of 'opening' the body, and the pleasure she takes in this. Another operation

> may take place in the Nikolaj Church in Denmark. I am working on my operating theatre suite, which will be a two-way mirror sculpture 8m x 6m, looking like a combination of an egg and an irregularly cut diamond. The operation will take place in public in a gallery of contemporary art. This operation won't be a cosmetic one, but one which will considerably alter my appearance, and whose aim will be to enhance my physical faculties (Orlan 1998a: 100)

Although the second of these surgeries could be quite complex and medically dangerous, and conforms closely to the idea of self-reinvention at the core of 'Reincarnation', neither of them adds meaningfully to its artistic programme. If Orlan goes ahead with them, they will be only loosely related to 'Reincarnation's structure, and will certainly not constitute its finale or conclusion.

'Reincarnation' is an open-ended project, one whose temporal end-point remains uncertain. In my view, this open-endedness and uncertainty are necessary, not contingent, features of the project. The *time* of the project has been evidenced by its uncertain, halting rhythm, in which intense phases of surgical activity have alternated with longish inactive lulls – which are nonetheless still integral parts of it. The operations constitute the acts of the project, but its main emphasis, I want to argue in the rest of this chapter, is on flux, transformation, and process. This relates back to the debates about modernist versus postmodernist performance already discussed. In the suspiciously binary table opposing features of modernism and postmodernism offered in a 1980 essay by Ihab Hassan, process/performance/happening is proposed as postmodernism's opposition to modernism's art object/finished work (Hassan 1980: 123).

Saint Orlan's reincarnation (as?) will never be definitively complete: her surgical self-transformation is not work *on* identity, but a work *of* identity (a *'travail d'identité'*), work in which she is engaged with her entire artistic persona – which does not necessarily detract from her agency as an artist and her control over the direction the project takes. In embarking upon the progressive surgical alteration of her appearance, Orlan did not just set herself a model to emulate, a visual goal that she could achieve within a fixed period of time, even although she did design a fixed template for her surgeons to work from. What she did was to find in a controversial contemporary medical practice a kind of allegory for the way in which finite human subjectivity can continue to modify itself, materially and endlessly.

Performing Performativity

The links of performance to performativity make up an area that linguistics, philosophy and gender theory have recently begun to consider closely. In this section I shall look in turn at performance and performativity as they relate to 'Reincarnation', firstly to the bodily dimension of the project, and secondly to text, by which I mean the readings Orlan makes during her operation-performances. I shall then consider the intersection of performance and performativity in Orlan's work, and attempt to draw some general conclusions about what kind of relationship we should be attempting to see between these two concepts in contemporary performance studies.

Orlan's treatment of her body, as has been made obvious by the amount of attention and commentary 'Reincarnation' has received since 1990, raises issues central to an understanding of the female body in contemporary

Western culture. One interpretation one might make of the way her body is being invaded and reinvented by the forces of technology and medicine, is that she is a textbook example of the account of the body to be found in the work of Foucault, whereby sex and bodies can be seen as social productions rather than as material ones. (Credit for the application of this idea to women's bodies should really go not to Foucault, who is notoriously silent about the question of gender, but to the feminist critics who have taken up and developed his ideas.) According to Foucault bodies are entirely at the mercy of power exercised within social relations; they are the products of cultural forces and discourses. In Orlan's case the discourse as well as the technology of medicine is reshaping her body, along with the discourses of the disciplines of art, art history and fashion.

Foucault's ideas seem very pertinent to Orlan's artistic practice. It would be possible to argue that she exemplifies the exhaustive influence and control of discourses and cultural forces over the body, the total suppression of what Foucaultian feminists call the 'pre-discursive' body, a natural or material body before it has been got at by social forces. However, the problem with the Foucaultian framework, ultimately, is that it maintains this rigid demarcation between the discursive and the (albeit non-existent) pre-discursive body, and, as a consequence of the opposition, the concept of a 'natural' pre-social, bio-logical body. This notion is one which theorists of gender such as Luce Irigaray and Judith Butler have recently been concerned to undo, or to show the con-structedness of. Both Irigaray's and Butler's readings of philosophical and contemporary theoretical texts draw attention to the constructedness of nature as a category. According to Irigaray and Butler – and this is an insight also to be found in Derridean deconstruction and in recent work by historians of science – there is no monolith 'matter', no biological bedrock. What Butler proposes instead 'is a return to the notion of matter, not as a site or surface, but as *a process of materialization that stabilizes over time to produce the effect of boundary, fixity and surface we call matter*'(Butler 1993: 9). In my view it is this emphasis on materialization rather than materiality, along with complementary critical writing on the posthuman body discussed in Chapter 3, which can offer us the most interesting insights into, and elucidation of, Orlan's work. What are we seeing in Orlan's performances other than materialization as a process, the slow, painstaking and apparently painful reshaping of matter? In *Bodies that Matter*, Butler suggests that the notion of materialization may offer a deconstructive alternative to the opposition of essentialism and constructivism that has come to constitute an impasse for some forms of feminist theory. Orlan's 'Reincarnation' project seems to offer a near-perfect illustration of this process of materialization, an open-ended transformation of body tissue brought out particularly in cosmetic surgery and other body modification practices.

Butler's theory of materialization is of a piece with the other main notion put forward in *Bodies that Matter* that has particular implications for thinking about the body, performativity, a notion that all commentators on performance seem to agree is especially pertinent to their field. Performativity can most readily be defined as the capacity of a linguistic utterance to bring about the action the utterance describes, or names (thus, the performative utterance 'I confess' is itself a confession). First broached by the linguist and speech act theorist John Austin, in lectures at Harvard in the 1950s which became his book *How to do things with words*, the extent and role of performativity in speech was an area quickly taken up by critics and theorists of theatre and performance. Most recently, the work of Judith Butler has introduced performativity into gender theory. Both Butler's books *Gender Trouble* (1990) and *Bodies that Matter* (1993) draw on speech act theory and on the debate which took place between Jacques Derrida and Austin's student and follower John Searle, later published in one volume as *Limited Inc.*, in order to construct a theory of gender performativity. According to this theory, gender norms are not laid down immutably in the manner of Lacan's law of the phallus, but are produced by their 'performance' within discourse. Butler uses Derrida's point against Searle, in which Derrida states that the felicitous functioning of performatives depends upon a certain kind of iterability or repeatability (a ship could not meaningfully be launched if the speech act 'I name this ship . . . may God bless her and all who sail in her' were not already a repetition or recitation of a previous such ceremony) to show how gender is produced by the repetition of performative acts.

Orlan's refashioning of her body undoubtedly provides a striking instance of Butler's theory of the continual displacement of the norms of identity via (re)materialization; does it also illustrate gender performativity? To return to my emphasis on the distinction of product from process, and the place of the operations as 'acts' within the process of Orlan's 'Reincarnation' project, it does seem possible to understand the different stages of the project as the repetitions which Butler sees as constituting gender performativity. Butler insists that the notion of performativity must be kept distinct from the notion of performance, because while the latter presumes a voluntarist conception of subjectivity according to which we can all theatrically remake, or restyle, our bodies and identities, the former, performativity, contests the very notion of the subject (Butler 1994: 33). The two concepts can and should be distinguished theoretically, but Orlan's surgical performance art calls upon them both simultaneously; she performs performativity **whilst** performativity performs her.

The relevance of performativity to the part played by Orlan's body in her performances is thus not hard to show. Action and transformation with material effects – transitivity – is incontestably going on. Whether the readings of texts she makes also function performatively raises more questions, and intervenes in more debates. This is because throughout the history of performance, whichever history is constructed, text has been an element whose necessity and importance has been much contested. Contemporary performance, as Marvin Carlson shows, is less interested in seeing itself as a cousin of literary forms and of drama as the heir to Aristotle's dramatic poetry than in tracing its connections with circus, the sideshow, or rap, to name but a few performance activities (Carlson 1996: 82). Carlson does also indicate that text is currently making something of a comeback, after a particularly experimental phase in the 1970s and 1980s in which it was usually eschewed.[7] But as Gérard Genette also observes, 'the work of performance 'proper' [. . .] is the performance event minus the text, just as Roland Barthes said: "theatricality is theatre minus the text"' (Genette 1994: 70).[8] A secondary or derivative status always threatens the linguistic or textual elements of performance.

In 'Reincarnation' Orlan reads from what appear to be very carefully chosen texts: a passage from psychoanalyst Eugénie Lemoine-Luccioni's book *La robe* which Lemoine-Luccioni wrote partly with Orlan in mind, excerpts from the work of the philosopher Michel Serres, and a well-known passage on abjection from Julia Kristeva's *Pouvoirs d'horreur/Powers of Horror*.[9] I would like to suggest that text and reading are important to Orlan's performances in at least the following ways. Firstly, the theoretical and intellectual character of the texts sends a strong message to her audience about how and in what context she wants her project to be understood – as theoretically significant, and in an intellectual rather than a popular context. Secondly, the act of reading aloud during her operations emphasizes Orlan's consciousness, which is linked in turn to two important aspects of 'Reincarnation'. Consciousness enables a display of detachment which reinforces irony and the parodic side of the project. And consciousness and activity (as well as detachment) show agency, which has to be demonstrated if Orlan's work is to be acknowledged as feminist.[10]

In my view these conclusions as to the importance of text and of the act of reading in Orlan's operations add up to more than a minor role, and perhaps

7. 'The initial emphasis on body and movement, with a general rejection of discursive language, has given way gradually to image-centred performance and a return of language' (Carlson 1996: 116)

8. 'L'oeuvre de performance proprement dite [. . .] c'est l'événement performanciel moins le texte, comme Roland Barthes disait: "la théâtralité, c'est le théâtre moins le texte".'

9. Other readings Orlan has used during her operation-performances include texts by Artaud (on the body-without-organs), Alphonse Allais, Raphaël Cuir, and Sanskrit texts from the Bagavazhita.

10. The feminist art critic Marsha Meskimmon comments as follows on the issue of control in 'Reincarnation'. 'The issue of control in the Orlan project is crucial because it alters the

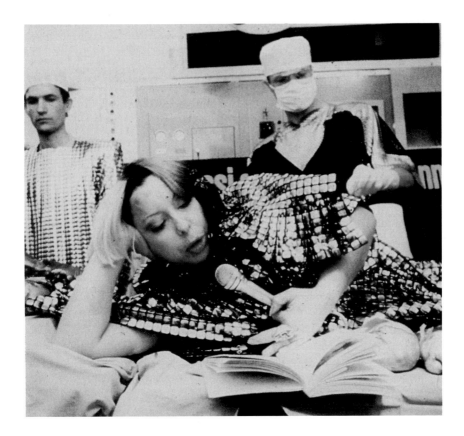

Figure 17. One of twelve operation 'details' in homage to all the mouths that have something to say, 4th operation-performance, 8 December 1990, Paris. Cibachrome in diasec vacuum, 165cm × 110cm. Photo by Joël Nicolas/Alain Dohmé for SIPA Press.

to a fully-fledged challenge to the traditional secondariness of text in performance. Do they demonstrate any performativity at work? The point from recent discussions of performativity that should be recalled here is Judith

---

subject/object relationship in the work. If she can be said to control the project, it could be a dynamic response to the technological possibilities available to people in the late twentieth century and the concepts of excessive femininity as masquerade. If, however, Orlan is the material of surgeons and the art establishment, her work is little more than a radical restaging of the traditional disempowerment of women in our society' (Meskimmon 1996: 127).

Butler's reminder of Derrida's deconstruction of the opposition between constative and performative speech acts, where constative speech acts are defined as those utterances which describe or observe, factually, without transitively affecting their objects or their environment. Butler's argument at this point relates to power and to subjectivity, but she says:

> To claim that discourse is formative is not to claim that it originates, causes or exhaustively composes that which it concedes; rather, it is to claim that there is no reference to a pure body which is not at the same time a further formation of that body. [. . .] In philosophical terms, the constative claim is always to some degree performative (Butler 1993: 10–11).

The content of the readings made by Orlan relates to her own body in performance. If I take the Kristeva extract from *Pouvoirs d'horreur* as an example, Orlan's recitation of Kristeva's description of the process of abjection – the formation of new bodily boundaries for subjectivity by means of the expulsion of matter, as occurs in liposuction – can be seen to be referring to *and therefore contributing to* the body-formation taking place. One non-surgical occasion on which Orlan read this extract was during the performance piece she devised for the ICA in London in April 1996, 'Woman with Head', which used techniques of illusion similar to those employed by professional magicians to present Orlan's head alone on a table, with no part of her body visible. (Reminiscent of Samuel Beckett's Winnie in the second act of *Happy Days*, buried up to her neck in sand, as well as of more popular forms of illusion-creating entertainment, such as a woman about to be sawn in half by a magician, whose head is the only part of her body protruding from the box through which she is to be sawn, this was a striking image.) The performative force of the Kristeva reading on this occasion would seem to have been the abjection or disavowal of the entire body, as pronounced by Orlan in her statement 'The body is obsolete'.

The Lemoine-Luccioni reading from *La robe* concerns the skin, and runs as follows:

> It is quite clear that the only possession he has ("my skin is all I have to my name" is a common expression) weighs heavily on him. It is still in excess, because having and being do not coincide, and because having is a cause of misunderstanding in all human relationships: I have the skin of an angel but I am a jackal, the skin of a crocodile, but I am a dog; a black skin but I am white; the skin of a woman but I am a man. I never have the skin of what I am. There is no exception to the rule because I am never what I have (Lemoine-Luccioni 1983: 95)

The disjuncture between having and being pinpointed here is one formulation of Orlan's divided subjectivity as both subject and object of her performance projects. And as I have shown in Chapter 1, Lemoine-Luccioni's focus on the skin, whose implication in questions of being she also draws attention to ('Skin deludes [. . .] But it does nonetheless suggest something to do with being' (ibid.)) suggests that the role played by the skin in body art, both as decoratable surface and as the very border or limit of the body, transforms and hugely enhances our understanding of the part played by the skin in the formation of personal identity.

The third important author from whom Orlan has read during her operation-performances is Michel Serres, and the passage of his work she has most often used is the following one, from *Le Tiers-instruit*:

> what can the common monster, tattooed ambidextrous, hermaphrodite and cross-bred, show to us right now under his skin? Yes, blood and flesh. Science talks of organs, functions, cells and molecules to acknowledge that it is high time that one stopped talking of life in the laboratories but science never utters the word flesh which, quite precisely, points out the mixtures in given place of the body, here and now, of muscles and blood, of skin and hair, of bones, nerves and of the various functions and which hence mixes up that which is analyzed by the discerning knowledge.[11]

This fascinating passage again refers to the skin, and to monstrosity. But its main theme is the challenge to science mounted by the flesh, both as raw bloody matter and as a word science does not 'dare' to use. Like the texts or readings by Kristeva and Lemoine-Luccioni, this passage refers doubly – both to Orlan's body and to the aims and implications of 'Reincarnation'. In view of this double reference, it is hard to regard these texts as purely constative speech acts that are simply neutrally describing Orlan's operations; much more convincing is Butler's claim that 'there is no reference to a pure body which is not at the same time a further formation of that body' (Butler 1993).

To return to the larger issue of the role of text and reading in performance art, one debate in twentieth-century performance has focused on the difference between the recitation of already existing (usually literary) passages that the performer interprets, and which are integrated with aspects of the numerous other arts which may be drawn upon, and the creation of an act or action in which text may or may not be involved (Carlson 1996: 92). In so far as her work fits both these descriptions, Orlan might be said to be contributing to an important debate in performance studies while simultaneously decon-structing some of its terms. If she is recombining traditionally opposed

11. Quoted in Hirschhorn 1996, p. 133, note 47.

characteristics of performance in new ways, this seems to be due to a considerable degree to the role given to text and to reading in her performances, which demonstrates a thorough inter-imbrication of performativity with performance, and of textuality with materiality.

Orlan's 'Reincarnation' project can, then, be seen to provide an excellent case study for the overlap between performativity and performance, what Andrew Parker and Eve Kosofsky Sedgwick have called an 'oblique intersection', 'one of the most fecund, as well as the most under-articulated' of the encounters of theoretical debates about performativity with other areas of cultural production (Parker and Sedgwick 1995: 1). Parker and Sedgwick's publication of a volume of papers from the 1993 English Studies conference devoted to performativity and performance indicates that performativity is indeed proving to be a fertile line of enquiry for critics of literature, drama and art, and Carlson's introduction to performance studies cites work by Ross Chambers and Umberto Eco that has deployed speech act theory, in particular, to analyse the relationship between actor/performer and audience. A reminder is sounded early in Parker and Sedgwick's introduction to their volume that it was Derrida's essay on Austin's theory of performative speech acts, 'Signature Event Context', that vitally confronted the opposition between 'literary' and 'ordinary' language. As they say, 'Where Austin [. . .] seemed intent on separating the actor's citational practice from ordinary speech-act performances, Derrida regarded both as structured by a generalized iterability, a pervasive theatricality common to stage and world alike' (ibid.: 4). My feeling is that this debt to deconstruction should be more fully acknowledged, because the undoing of the rigid opposition between 'theatrical' and 'political' speech, as well as the deconstruction of the distinction between stage-space and 'real-world' space (the latter implicit in the distinction of theatre from performance, but rarely given such precise focus) seems to have breached an important new area of research into the relationship of the aesthetic and the political. Is 'performance' turning out to be as important a paradigm to cultural studies as 'text' has proven to be in literary and theoretical studies? If so, it is one which requires rigorous argument and careful articulation. Marvin Carlson, whose study details the rise of performance as a concept in ethnography, anthropology, sociology and psychology, in fact sounds the following warning about the power of performativity as a paradigm for performance studies: 'When the very structure of the performative situation is recognized as already involved in the operations of the dominant social systems, directly oppositional performance becomes highly suspect, since there is no "outside" from which it can operate' (Carlson 1996: 172). Orlan is an artist who makes overtly political claims about her artistic practice ('Art can, art must change the world, it's its only justification' (Orlan 1996: 85).

The risk in over-emphasizing the importance of performativity to 'Reincarnation' is that the political force of the concept might drown out the rootedness of her diverse work in the avant-garde tradition of twentieth-century art, a tradition in relation to which European (as opposed to American) performance art has traced its short but fascinating history.

Cosmetic Surgery and the Feminist Performative Reconstruction of Female Subjectivity

Although she already probably ranked as France's most important performance artist by the late 1980s, it is really only since she began 'The Reincarnation of Saint Orlan' in 1990 that Orlan has gained international renown. As a consequence of this international recognition, critics and commentators of performance, their interest attracted and held by 'Reincarnation', have recently begun to turn their attention to earlier parts of Orlan's career, in order to trace connections between her 1970s and 1980s performances and exhibitions and the multiple concerns of her surgical work; perhaps the best example of this genealogical type of analysis is the substantial essay by Tanya Augsburg in the recent volume of papers from the First Annual Performance Studies Conference held in New York City in 1995, edited by Peggy Phelan and Jill Lane.[12] 'Reincarnation' has made Orlan as 'mainstream' to international performance as she has become to postmodern body politics, as is also indicated by the half-chapter devoted to her by the leading critic of postmodern performance Philip Auslander, in his book *From Acting to Performance: Essays in Modernism and Postmodernism*.[13] Augsburg's and Auslander's excellent essays are evidence of the centrality Orlan has acquired to performance studies, and it was perhaps to be expected that this would be the field in which her reputation would grow the fastest. What is also striking about the attention 'Reincarnation' has attracted is the range of subjects and disciplines from which it has come – visual arts, again perhaps predictably, but also psychoanalysis, philosophy, sociology and women's studies, in readings by Parveen Adams, Peggy Zeglin Brand and Kathy Davis.

12. *The Ends of Performance* (New York and London: New York University Press, 1998). Orlan appeared at this important inaugural conference of what has become Performance Studies international (PSi), and a version of Orlan's 'Conférence' entitled 'Intervention' appears in the volume after Augsburg's essay, 'Orlan's Performative Transformations of Subjectivity', pp. 315–27 and pp. 285–314 respectively.

13. 'The surgical self: body alteration and identity', on Orlan and Kate Bornstein, pp. 126–40, first published as 'Orlan's Theatre of Operations' in *TheatreForum* 7 (1995).

In the final part of this chapter I shall concentrate on the core issues raised by 'Reincarnation' and already broached in my discussion of performance and performativity – subjectivity, gender, sexuality and the medical body. In so doing, I shall use the differently oriented readings by Adams, Davis and Brand to construct my account of what 'Reincarnation' can offer to the debates about the body, medicine and female subjectivity that have been so important to cultural studies and visual culture in the 1990s.

Parveen Adams' Lacanian reading of some of the pictures from Orlan's operation-performances, 'Operation Orlan', has perhaps been the most important contribution to theorizing femininity, or female subjectivity, as it is explored and dramatized in Orlan's work. Adams endorses Orlan's own description of herself as a 'woman-to-woman transsexual,'[14] and compares her surgical self-reinvention to the gender reassignment of male-to-female transsexuals. Drawing on Lacan's account of sexual relations in which the woman's body is coded as phallic, Adams says of transsexuals, 'frequently the urge to refiguration involves a wish not to become a woman, but to become The Woman' (Adams 1996: 144). According to Lacan's theory of femininity, universal female subjectivity is an unattainable position; this is why he crosses out the 'La' of 'La Femme' in the title of the section on feminine *jouissance* (sexual pleasure) in his seminar on female sexuality, 'Encore' (Lacan 1975: 61). 'The Woman' is an identity only available – to persons of either sex – in phantasy, since occupying the position of The Woman means becoming the phallus, achieving the authority of sexual identity that only identification with the phallic signifer can confer. According to Adams, this phantasized phallic state of totalization is what male-to-female transsexuals are aiming at through their surgery. Transsexual desire targets an impossible, sexually undifferentiated completeness; 'it can be thought of as turning the knife against castration' (Adams 1996: 144). For Lacan and for Adams, the wish to be The Woman/the Phallus is part of a 'psychotic strain in the denial of sexual difference' (ibid.); 'in Lacanian terms the desire to be The Woman must be bound up with the fending-off of psychosis' (ibid.).

Although I do think that the surgery undergone by transsexuals as part of their gender reassignment can be compared with 'Reincarnation', a parallel between Orlan's desire and the desire of male-to-female transsexuals seems, at the least, problematic. Whatever the actual outcome of male-to-female transsexual surgery, which often does not equip its patient with the fully

---

14. 'I say that I am doing a woman-woman transsexualism by alluding to transsexuals: a man who feels himself to be a woman wants others to see: woman. We could summarise this by saying that it is a problem of communication' (Orlan 1996: 88).

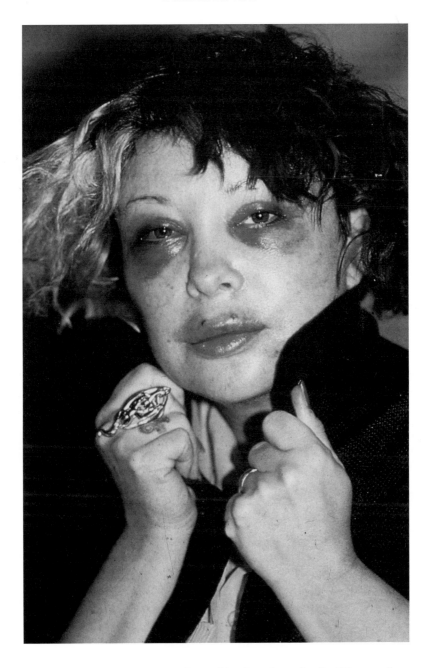

Figure 18. Portrait made by the body-machine four days after the 7th operation-
performance 'Omnipresence', New York, 21 November 1993.
Cibachrome in diasec vacuum, 110cm × 240cm. Photo by Vladimir
Sichov for SIPA Press.

Figure 19. 'Women look like the moon and my eyes like flowers', or self-portrait with narcissi. Portrait made by the body-machine six days after the 7th operation-performance 'Omnipresence', New York, 21 November 1993. Cibachrome in diasec vacuum, 110cm × 240cm. Photo by Vladimir Sichov for SIPA Press.

functioning set of female sexual organs s/he hoped to acquire, its imagined course is a journey, or narrative, with a certain goal – physical female identity, and the state of being viewed and related to as a woman by society at large. Orlan's surgical project, as I have argued above, does not conform to 'closure' models of narrative; it does not have – or no longer has – a certain, knowable end, even imaginarily. Secondly, by employing Lacan's notion that The Woman is a position only available in phantasy, Adams' description of the desire of male-to-female transsexuals – and by extension, the desire behind Orlan's wish to transform her appearance through surgery – preserves intact the notion that there is a fixed, ahistorical ideal of femininity or female beauty governing the construction of that gender. I have emphasized at a number of points in this study that Orlan is not concerned to arrive by means of surgical mimesis at any one particular ideal of femininity; that the composite computer-generated image that has guided her surgeons deconstructs this aesthetic of unity. In sum, 'Reincarnation' is incompatible with any theory of female subjectivity that entertains a universalist, phallogocentric concept of The Woman. Although Adams concedes that Orlan 'works differently' from male-to-female transsexuals, she still employs the same Lacanian framework of sexual relations, in which the woman's body is seen as phallic, to elucidate Orlan's work.

A performance Orlan did in the Louvre in Paris in 1978 in fact illustrates her familiarity with, and yet critical distance from, the Freudo-Lacanian concept of the phallic woman (and thus reinforces the deconstruction of 'phallic' spectatorship implied in her documentary study of the Medusa, as I argued it in Chapter 2). The context of this performance was Orlan's acting out of the 'penis-as paintbrush' metaphor as interpreted by Tanya Augsburg and quoted alongside my reading of Orlan's 'invagination' of the body with dress in Chapter 1. A momentary part of Orlan's appropriation of this metaphor, which she achieved by displaying, in profile, an 'erect' paintbrush re-covering her shorn pubis through a white artist's palette, was the display of an image of a phallic woman. As Augsburg puts it (although her reading seems still to conform to the phallogocentric conception of the female body as phallic which I have just critiqued in Parveen Adams's reading of Orlan's art),

> Alternatively, Orlan restaged the scene of castration by displaying her lack of a penis only to follow the display with a compensatory, showy simulation of the phallus. For a brief instant Orlan unveiled what could be called "an impossible figure of totality", in which she presented herself as both being and having the phallus. [. . .] The fleeting transience of the figurative image also marks performance as fantasy, which is why Orlan's performative presentation of a fantasy of artistic fulfillment could last but a moment.' (Augsburg 1998: 295–6)

To return to my critique of Parveen Adams's phallogocentric reading of Orlan's femininity and desire, my rejection of Adams's Lacanian version of Orlan's 'woman-to-woman transsexualism' is not meant to suggest that 'Reincarnation' entails no process of 'becoming-woman'. The alternative interpretation of Orlan's self-designation as a 'woman-to-woman transsexual' I would put forward is that the femaleness towards which Orlan's surgical project shows her to be moving is a subjectivity unfamiliar to the Western sociosymbolic order, a 'femininity' that is not determined by phallocentric law or grounded in Western metaphysics. Like Gladys Fabre, who suggests that we can see in the alternation between the personae of the white and black virgins performed by Saint Orlan in the 1980s a 'war' the black virgin is gradually winning, and the 'metaphysical death' of the white virgin – the passive, static femininity of Christian logocentrism (Fabre 1984: 6) – I believe that Orlan's surgical 'transsexualism' marks the passage – a vital moment for Western societies and culture – from the sociosymbolic entrapment of femininity theorized by Western metaphysics into a performativity of sexualities and genders that will be very different in the twenty-first century. The enormously influential theory of gender performativity put forward by Judith Butler in *Gender Trouble* and *Bodies that Matter* breaks open the prison-house of the Lacanian Symbolic order by deconstructing its founding terms, and sets out the parameters for a scene of plural and modifiable gender identities not harnessed to the binary ideals of masculinity and femininity theorized by psychoanalysis, even if psychoanalysis constantly tells us men and women never actually match up to those ideals.

Like Butler's theory of gender performativity, Orlan's surgical practice works to expose and circumvent the formative and *normative* power of a psychoanalytic gendered ideal of femininity – an ideal Orlan herself has repeatedly insisted she is not in quest of. However, although Judith Butler's work has had far-reaching negative effects on the contribution of Lacanian psychoanalysis to feminist gender theory, it certainly does not write off psychoanalysis as a discourse. According to Butler, psychic identification and incorporation as theorized by Freud are mechanisms central to the formation of gender identity. In the section of *Gender Trouble* entitled 'Freud and the Melancholia of Gender', Butler underlines the importance of Freud's insight that the mechanism of melancholia, which involves the subject's identification with a lost love-object, is essential to the very formation of the ego. In 'The Ego and the Id', Freud emphasizes that his earlier essay 'Mourning and Melancholia'did not appreciate the full significance' of the mechanism by which an object-cathexis is replaced by an identification. The mechanism, he stresses in the later essay, is common, typical, and 'has a great share in determining the form taken by the ego [. . .] mak[ing] an essential contribution towards building up what is called its "character"'(Freud, quoted in Butler 1990: 58). The ego, in other words, gains its very nature from loving and losing: it is a 'precipitate of abandoned object-cathexes and [. . .] contains the history of those object-choices' (ibid.). The means by which the ego is constructed – and crucially, by which gender identity is acquired – is a quasi-oral internalization or 'introjection' of abandoned love-objects. Freud only alludes to the centrality of melancholia to the construction of gender identity (ibid.: 57), but Butler explores and develops an account of the accretion of the gendered ego through the oral mechanisms of identification and introjection.

My reason for delving further into Butler's theory of the formation of gender identity at this point is that it seems to me that her account of the part played by melancholic psychic mechanisms in the formation of gender offers a compelling explanation of Orlan's relationship with the female icons whose features she has had inscribed into her flesh during 'Reincarnation'. Orlan chose the Mona Lisa, Botticelli's Venus, Diana, Psyche and Europa as the icons from which to compose her new identity as a woman because she loved their images. She did not want to resemble them visually, but she admired and wanted to associate herself with their qualities of character – androgyny, carnal beauty, temerity and aggressivity, fragility and vulnerability, and fascination by adventure and the future. To Orlan, her female icons were (homosexual) love-objects she could not personally know, but who have certainly played a part in the ongoing construction of her identity as a woman. In having a facial feature of each icon sculpted into her flesh, Orlan found a visual means of inscribing and displaying her always-already lost love for some of the heroines of Western art history.

The above account of why Orlan's 'Reincarnation' project makes an important contribution to feminist theories of female subjectivity at the end of the twentieth century has said very little about the project's relationship to cosmetic surgery as a medical practice. To close this final chapter I shall try to make good this omission by discussing the reading of 'Reincarnation' made by Kathy Davis, a sociologist working in Women's Studies at the University of Utrecht whose recent study of cosmetic surgery, *Reshaping the Female Body: The Dilemma of Cosmetic Surgery*, is the fullest feminist analysis yet written of this controversial medical practice. Davis's response to Orlan's involvement in cosmetic surgery was published two years after *Reshaping the Female Body*, and in it she explains how she came to find herself writing about an experimental feminist artist:

Given my research on cosmetic surgery, I was obviously intrigued by Orlan's surgical experiments. While I was fascinated by her willingness to put her body under the knife, however, I did not immediately see what her project had to offer for understanding why 'ordinary' women have cosmetic surgery.[. . .] It came as a surprise, therefore, when my research was continually being linked to Orlan's project. Friends and colleagues sent me clippings about Orlan. At lectures about my work, I was invariably asked what I thought about Orlan. Journalists juxtaposed interviews with me and Orlan for their radio programmes or discussed us in the same breath in their newspaper pieces. Our projects were cited as similar in their celebration of women's agency and our insistence that cosmetic surgery was about more than beauty (ibid.: 169–70).

Repeated comparisons of her own work with Orlan's eventually led Davis to reconsider her scepticism about 'Reincarnation''s relationship to the experiences of most women who undergo cosmetic surgery, and one of the two questions she consequently sets out to address in 'My Body is My Art' is 'to what extent Orlan's aims coincide with my own; that is, to provide a feminist critique of the technologies and practices of the feminine beauty system while taking women who have cosmetic surgery seriously' (ibid.: 170).

In response to this question Davis notes several similarities between Orlan's stated reasons for having cosmetic surgery and the motivations described by the female surgical patients she interviewed for *Reshaping the Female Body*. Neither Orlan nor Davis's interviewees were interested in becoming more beautiful, and both Orlan and the women Davis spoke with 'viewed them-selves as agents who, by remaking their bodies, remade their lives as well' (ibid.: 175). Davis's 'ordinary' women rejected the idea that by going under the knife, they were being coerced or manipulated by social and ideological forces; they embarked upon surgery as thoroughgoing agents, seeing it as a way of taking control over their lives, their bodies and their happiness. After noting these important similarities between Orlan and her interviewees, however, Davis abruptly changes tack.

[T]his is where the similarities end. Orlan's project is not about a real-life problem; it is about art.[. . .] Her body is little more than a vehicle for her art and her personal feelings are entirely irrelevant (ibid.: 175–6).

It is hard to imagine a more wrongheaded approach to Orlan's work than this. What artist can be said to be this indifferent to and uninvolved with their work? Surely not one who has undergone nine surgeries and permanently altered her appearance in its service. Since she is a body artist, it is accurate to say that Orlan's body is her vehicle, but it is also still a material entity from which her personal identity is inseparable. And it is clear from Orlan's numerous statements about her surgical work that her personal feelings *are* relevant; it is important, for instance, that her spectators see the great pleasure she takes in being operated upon, as well as the degree of pain she will admit to. Davis can in fact only disable the comparison between Orlan and the majority of women who have cosmetic surgery by imposing a rigid binary opposition between art and reality, or art and life, that is wholly inappropriate to Orlan as well as to most – perhaps all – body art, whose practitioners are a particularly 'autobiographical' brand of artist. Orlan's 'Reincarnation' project is most certainly public and political, but her motivation for undertaking it was also, I am convinced, as private and personal as the motivation of the thousands of women who now opt each year to have liposuction, breast enhancement or a face-lift.[15]

By asserting that 'Reincarnation' has nothing to do with 'real life' and that Orlan is not emotionally involved in the project, though, Davis opens up a connection with the important reading of Orlan's surgical work made by philosopher Peggy Zeglin Brand, in 'Disinterestedness and Political Art' (Brand 1998). Davis begins her article by recounting how a young female spectator at a presentation Orlan gave to an Amsterdam multimedia festival in 1995, irritated by the way Orlan lectured through a projected film of surgery rather than commenting on the shocking images being shown, finally 'stood up and exclaimed "You act as though it were not *you*, up there on the screen"' (ibid.: 168). Davis comments 'Here is a woman whose face has been mutilated and yet discusses it intellectually and dispassionately. The audience is squirming and Orlan is acting as though she were not directly involved' (ibid.). Orlan stands accused here of excessive emotional detachment from – a disinterested response to – her own self-images, and of apparently expecting the same type of response from her spectators. In the light of comments Orlan has made and published about watching images from 'Reincarnation', this seems fair enough.[16] The young female spectator, whose reaction Davis

---

15. The genesis of Orlan's bodily reincarnation via cosmetic surgery also belies the kind of totally unfeeling relationship to her work Davis suggests, as the idea of turning surgical interventions into performance art first occurred to Orlan in 1978, when she was operated on for an extra-uterine pregnancy under a local anaesthetic. 'Due to speak at a symposium in New York, she felt ill, needed emergency surgery and decided to take a video crew along. The resulting tape was immediately rushed across town and shown in her place at the symposium' (McClellan 1994: 40). There was a degree of chance at the origin of the work, but since the life of a foetus was at stake, even if its chances of survival were minimal, 'Reincarnation' has its roots in a highly personal and (presumably) emotionally charged moment in Orlan's life.

16. 'When watching these images, I suggest that you do what you probably do when you watch the news on television. It is a question of not letting yourself be affected by the images, and of continuing to reflect upon them' (Orlan 1996: 84).

defends, 'may simply be concerned that in order to appreciate art, she is being required to dismiss her own feelings' (ibid.: 179). Peggy Brand opens her article with the question 'Can an ordinary viewer ever experience art – particularly politically charged, socially relevant art – in a neutral, detached, and objective way?' (Brand 1998: 155), and goes on to argue for an approach to the viewing of art that combines the traditional disinterested spectatorship recommended by eighteenth- and nineteenth-century aesthetic theory with the 'interested' viewing necessarily advocated by later political critics of art, such as feminist art critics. For Brand, Orlan's 'Reincarnation' project, which she discusses alongside an Ingres painting called 'La Source' much commented on by traditional philosophical art critics, is really just a particularly good example of provocative contemporary feminist art. But her advocacy of an approach to the viewing of art that 'toggles' between what she calls IA (interested attention) and DA (disinterested attention) – an oscillation that she suggests may or may not be conscious and deliberate – represents a valuable attempt to bring together traditional universalist aesthetic theory, the psychology of perception, and politically informed art criticism, and in a way that can provide a meaningful account of the disinterest Orlan displays to her surgical self-images, and sometimes recommends to her spectators as a viewing technique they should try.

Returning now to Kathy Davis's argument about 'Reincarnation'; although Davis does go on to say, after her divorce of Orlan's art from any 'real-life', felt, human involvement with cosmetic surgery, that it may be 'overhasty' (Davis 1997: 176) to dismiss comparisons between Orlan's surgical experiences and those of most women who have cosmetic surgery, and although she then reconsiders the relevance of what she terms 'utopian' approaches to surgery (this includes Orlan's) to her own investigation of women's lives, she enumerates four aspects of such approaches that she says make her uneasy. She accuses utopian visions of what cosmetic surgery can achieve of the following: firstly, of discounting the suffering of surgery; secondly, of discounting the risks that surgery involves; thirdly, of ignoring women's suffering with their appearance; and fourthly, of discounting 'the everyday acts of compliance and resistance which are part of ordinary women's involvement in cosmetic surgery' (ibid.: 179). I have already responded fully to the first two of these accusations in earlier chapters, by arguing that disavowal of suffering is an important part of the complex social masochism of 'Reincarnation', and that risk is a real and significant dimension of Orlan's surgical practice. As regards Davis's third accusation, I concede that Orlan is not particularly preoccupied with women's suffering with their appearance (although she undoubtedly sympathizes with it), but would argue that Orlan's self-transformation *away* from a pleasing womanly appearance towards a less well-proportioned face gives an important critical twist to the conventional suffering of women who choose to have cosmetic surgery. Orlan's affirmation that 'Reincarnation' has made her body a site of public debate about the pressures exerted by patriarchal society on the objectifiable female body suggests that before electing to have surgery, she felt too 'pretty', too feminine, too much of an image. Transforming her face has been a way of repairing an alienation from her conventionally feminine appearance, a way of bringing the way she is perceived by the world into line with her interior sense of self. As regards Davis's fourth accusation about utopian approaches to cosmetic surgery discounting 'the everyday acts of compliance and resistance which are part of ordinary women's involvement in cosmetic surgery' (ibid.), I will say simply that despite her artistic extraordinariness, Orlan has been subject to the same difficulties and reversals that other women undergo on the operating table, and has had to have corrective surgery on at least one occasion.

Despite retracting to some extent her pronouncement that 'Reincarnation' is not about 'a real-life problem' and that Orlan's personal feelings 'are entirely irrelevant', Davis concludes her article by stating unambiguously that such utopian approaches to surgery leave out 'the sentient and embodied female subject, the one who feels concern about herself and about others' (ibid.: 180). Orlan is not Mother Theresa, and she may engage to a considerable extent, as I have argued in Chapter 3, with discourses of posthumanity, but she is undoubtedly a 'sentient and embodied female subject', one whose life and art work are interrelated in a complex but particularly interesting way; a woman who has changed and matured over the years 'The Reincarnation of Saint Orlan' has taken. In the conclusion to the book which follows this chapter, I shall return to this genealogy of Orlan's life and art, and develop further my reading of who Orlan is, and who she has been becoming.

Conclusion: The Millennial Female

One of Orlan's most intriguing and revealing statements about her own sense of her identity has been that as a child and an adolescent, she did not recognize herself by her image in the mirror. Rather than as any considered comment on Lacan's concept of the *stade du miroir*, this statement should perhaps be understood as the expression of a profound experience of alienation from her external appearance: a radical disjuncture between that appearance and the internal sense of who she is that we all, as self-conscious human beings, carry within us at every waking moment. It is this type of alienation from their appearance that seems to exist among certain patients of cosmetic surgery, and has recently begun to come under medical scrutiny, acquiring for itself the technical-sounding name of Body Dysmorphic Disorder, or BDD ('dysmorphic' because 'sufferers' of the condition do not identify with the shape that their body image presents to them, and – typically at least – imagine certain features of the image to be far larger or smaller, more distorted or less pleasing to look at than they actually are). In Orlan's case, as I suggested in Chapter 4, the dynamic of displeasure with appearance seems to be reversed (although her sense of alienation from it is no less profound), since rather than seeking to 'improve' her external appearance to bring it in line with a desire to look 'good' (= well-proportioned, in classical theories of beauty), she has altered it in conformity with her desire for artistic experiment, and, while making it look (in the eyes of most observers) somewhat *less* pleasing, has not been displeased with the result.

This kind of alienation from one's external appearance is already implied in the passage about the skin from Eugénie Lemoine-Luccioni's *La robe* Orlan has read from during operation-performances, and from which I have quoted more than once. The disjuncture between 'having' and 'being' Lemoine-Luccioni describes is tantamount to saying, as Malgorzata Lisiewicz also does when she writes of Orlan's work that '[t]he body is a place where "the signified" and "the signifying" [sic] never manage to reach' (Lisiewicz 1996: 50), that one's external appearance is something one can never possess. We cannot own the way we look because our external appearance is always and irremediably in the domain of the Other, the realm of social relations where so much depends (not always desirably of course) on the appearance we present to the world. Appearance may even be said to belong to the Other, in so far as decisions are made and actions taken by other people that hugely influence our life-trajectories as subjects, based on the way we look.

But the alienation from her appearance Orlan describes (and which, interestingly, she says does not extend to her voice, which has remained a means of self-recognition throughout her sequence of cosmetic surgeries)[1] is, like Lemoine-Luccioni's identification of the disjuncture between having and being, another formulation of the splitting of the subject theorized by psychoanalysis, the split between the conscious and the unconscious mind, but also between the acting, voluntarist subject and the unfree, social one. The main way in which this splitting has been dramatized in Orlan's work is of course in her double role in the operating theatre, as both 'passive' patient of the surgery she undergoes, and conscious director and choreographer of the filming and performance going on, as well its leading player – really a multiple rather than a double role. It is my contention, though, that in her surgical project the influence of Orlan's splitness as a subject is more extensive even than this. My view, in other words – contrary to the insistences of commentators who say she is not personally or emotionally involved in the work – is that Orlan's desire has been very much at stake in 'Reincarnation', that the project has marked a kind of rite of passage for her, and enabled her to be more at ease with her professional ambition and her social relationships as well as with her appearance. In more psychoanalytic terms – those I proposed very early in this study when using the ideas of Luce Irigaray and Christine Battersby to interpret Orlan's public body-measurings – the symbolization of products of Orlan's imaginary can be seen in the representational structures of 'Reincarnation'. 'Representational structures' in this instance means the very practice-upon-the-self that cosmetic surgery has come to emblematize for contemporary Western societies in recent years.

The particular suggestion I want to make about Orlan's surgical self-reconstruction here, following the idea that 'Reincarnation' can be understood as a kind of bodily psychoanalysis, is one also made by Tanya Augsburg, although reached by Augsburg via a different route. It is that the much-noted and sometimes upsetting distance Orlan takes from the emotional upheaval of undergoing surgery (discussed in Chapter 4 by referring to Peggy Brand's aesthetical notion of disinterested spectatorship) is possible because her surgery is ultimately an action she is carrying out upon herself, in which

1. 'my voice is my security', in conversation with me in Paris, August 1998.

the surgeon's scalpel stands in for her reflective consciousness. Orlan's extraordinary lucidity about what is at stake in her operation-performances is evidence that, although she is unquestionably highly invested in her surgery at an unconscious level, she is also set upon self-transformation in a highly conscious manner. Like a sharp razor, her consciousness cuts herself, creating wounds which become new sites for self-reflection, as well as for the reflection of others (Augsburg 1998: 304).

This demonstrated self-consciousness by a woman has significant theoretical implications. Orlan's crystal-clear and unemotional explanations of the effects aimed at by 'Reincarnation', distributed in her 'Conférence' at each presentation of the project, show her to be a type of subject that logocentric (particularly Hegelian) philosophy of subjectivity says cannot exist – a self-conscious feminine subject (a 'Woman with Head'). This is a subjectivity that cannot be, and will never be able to be, straightforwardly represented in the terms and language of metaphysical philosophy. It can, however, be alluded to and performed in the interstices of logocentric representational structures, and this is the tension and paradoxicality that can be discerned and felt behind much of Orlan's work – for example, in the finite-yet-infinite temporality of 'Reincarnation'. The effort detectable behind many of Orlan's earlier artistic projects, as well as behind the self-reinvention explicitly thematized in 'Reincarnation', is the effort to be born anew as a kind of female subject that has never existed – or not existed since a pre-patriarchal era. A crucial ambiguity about the striving to give birth to this post-patriarchal woman (as well as to be born *as* her) is whether it means Orlan becomes her own mother (replacing the hated real-life mother by giving birth to herself) or whether, as Bernard Ceysson notes (Ceysson 1990: 15), it is equivalent to the birth of a daughter who has no mother – a kind of divine or miraculous birth.

With these questions of a female divine and female genealogies, reinforced as they are by the influence Orlan's unsatisfactory and impeding relationship with her own mother has had on her career – an influence expressed in many of her artistic projects – Orlan's *oeuvre* runs up once more against the limits of phallogocentric structures of representation. The work of Luce Irigaray and other feminist philosophers has shown that the construction of female genealogies – same-generational or cross-generational female relationships that involve three or more women, and thus cannot be subject to the imprisoning dynamics of unmediated, dyadic relations between mothers and their daughters – are a vital step women must take if they are to break open the confines of patriarchy, and move beyond it into more enabling terrain. But the more immediately arresting aspect of Orlan's attempts to be reborn as a post-patriarchal female (the millennial female) is the project of self-reinvention they entail, which echoes similar efforts by many well-known writers and artists, none more suggestive for Orlan's work than Antonin Artaud, who became 'creatively preoccupied with the project of reformulating his identity' shortly after he was first interned in 1937 (Barber 1993: 97), and in August 1939 rebaptized himself Antonin Nalpas (Nalpas was his mother's maiden name), reneged completely on his former social identity, and went on to create for himself a new mythological family of 'daughters of the heart to be born' (ibid.: 102). Naming and renaming is an important dimension of Orlan's projects of self-reinvention, and one I shall now consider more closely than I have done so far, as part of this concluding overview of Orlan's life as an artist.

In the entire issue that the French medical journal *VST* devoted to Orlan in 1991, which also contains the interesting psychiatric report filed on her by a Dr O. Relandt,[2] one article considers the question of naming from a psychiatric and philosophical point of view.[3] Starting with the Bible, and with the story of the creation of the world told in the book of Genesis, Patrice Desmons observes that although God created the world, He left the 'dirty job' of naming all animals and plants to Adam – in other words, to mankind. Man himself is named by God, since Judeo-Christian thought makes no allowance for self-naming, which *outside an artistic context* counts as a sacrilegious act in religious terms, and a psychotic act in psychiatric ones. Based on the hypothesis that the Genesis myth contains an entire theory of the sign and the image, Desmons explains that the structure of this myth is what lies behind the commandment 'Thou shalt not take God's name in vain'. God's name, Jaweh, means 'I am He who is'; it is an 'ideal, self-referential, but divine, inhuman' name (Desmons 1991: 40), the kind of name Man can never have, since a kind of secondary (unarticulated) commandment to the one about not taking God's name in vain is 'thou shalt not attribute to yourself your own name, which you will always receive from an Other' (ibid.). The transcendental ineffability of God's name is part of a structure of original debt that exists around naming, since the original split between the Creator and the act of naming (God and Man) creates a debt that subsequent acts of

2. 'Expertise psychiatrique d'une oeuvre d'art: Orlan', *VST* 23-24 sept–déc 1991, 43–5. The main diagnosis made is of 'artistic monomania', with secondary observations of extreme narcissism, depressive tendencies, and a 'pathology of freedom' (freedom from the identity – name and image – conferred upon her by her family and upbringing). To treat Orlan's 'monomania' would be equivalent to trying to cure her of her profession as an artist (p. 45), and her 'condition' is quite compatible with the exercising of a profession, and not a source of danger to anyone except herself.
3. Patrice Desmons, 'Noms de Dieu!', *VST* 23-24 sept–déc 1991, 40–2.

naming will always be trying to repair, in the nostalgic effort to return to the ideal, paradisiacal state of the name before the separation of the human from the divine.

According to the author of 'Noms de Dieu!' (the French expletive 'nom de Dieu!', uttered in place of the unspeakable name of God, itself betrays the refusal to respect the Law/the Other implied in the commandment), Orlan's self-naming – and I would specify additionally that this must apply to her original self-naming as Orlan in the early 1960s, as well as to the self-renaming projected for the end of 'Reincarnation' – constitutes a transgressive gesture of a similar kind to that represented by the expletive, as does the redesigning of her image in 'Reincarnation'. Orlan's gestures of auto-nomination effectively refuse to accept that her name be given by the/an Other. Instead, she demands that her name be produced – not given as a divine gift, but engendered (ibid.: 41). The name becomes a 'consequence' rather than an 'antecedence' (ibid.), the consequence of an artistic process, like the new body image Orlan began to acquire as soon as she started work on 'Reincarnation'. Orlan's non 'given' names are radically different to the ideal, self-referential name of God, that apparently arrives *ex nihilo* or *ex machina*. Her non-respect for the given name, like Artaud's,

> breaks with the traditional split that art has until now almost always respected [. . .]: a split between subject and object, between the author and the work.[. . .] To say something about this gesture of transformation and co-engendering of the image and the name [. . .] we have to break not only with the whole apparatus of metaphysical and religious interpretation, but also with the dualisms of subject/ object, self/other, human/divine, man/woman, eros/thanatos etc., which are the condition of production of psychiatric, psychopathological and psychoanalytic concepts'. (ibid.)

The production of Orlan is equivalent to the production of the work of art, which arises from the attempts to repair the debt incurred by the original split from the divine. Orlan is seeking not to become divine, which would be equivalent to replacing God and repairing the original split from which all artistic production follows, but to substitute for the debt thoroughgoing sacrilegious *jouissance* (ibid.: 42).

The sacrilegious gesture of refusing the given name, as now becomes clear, exactly parallels the 'blasphemy' Orlan claims for carnal art. As she notes in her manifesto of this new type of body art, and I discussed in Chapter 2, carnal art reverses the Christian and logocentric process by which the word becomes flesh, because in it, it is flesh that becomes word. Orlan's employment and reconstruction of her flesh, and the direct use of that flesh in works of art such as her reliquaries and the larger tablets of 'my flesh, the texts and the languages', is a resymbolization of the flesh (the body) that is both post-Christian and post-patriarchal – post-patriarchal because it is not just incidental that it is a woman's body that is being resymbolized in this way. Another vital reversal brought about by carnal art is, as both Parveen Adams and August Ruhs have noted, that of the age-old mimetic mechanism by which Art imitates Nature:

> Because with her (obviously very bold and to western culture exceedingly bold) actions she also proclaims a permanent overlordship belonging to art struggling to dissolve the position of the real by reversing the conditions of mimesis: Nature (here the nature of human body-tissue) must be forced to adapt itself to highly specific ideal shapes – as provided by art (Ruhs 1996: 155).

Challenging the logics of Christianity, patriarchy, and artistic mimesis, carnal art is literally and theoretically at the cutting edge of some of the most important problems and shifts faced by twentieth-century art, thought and culture.

My affirmation that carnal art is post-patriarchal presupposes that it is important that the flesh being (re)symbolized in Orlan's 'Reincarnation' project is female flesh (or the flesh of the female body). Here the questions raised by Orlan's work are once again identical with those of recent feminist philosophy; Luce Irigaray's insistence that the rethinking and reformation of the patriarchal Symbolic order depends upon a resymbolization of the feminine is a recurrent theme in her work from the 1970s onwards, as Margaret Whitford's ground-breaking study first clearly showed. One aspect of 'Reincarnation' particularly inflected by Orlan's femininity is its non-linear temporality, which, as the rich debates about *écriture féminine* and narrative have amply demonstrated in recent years, is characteristically 'feminine' in its non-teleological and cyclically inclined structure. But if debates about *écriture féminine* have tended repeatedly to run up against the impasse of essentialism (or the impasse constituted by the binary opposition of essentialism and constructivism), Orlan's carnal art takes debates about the female body into new, ethical territory. I would now like to look briefly at this ethical dimension of her work, before bringing my conclusion to a close with a discussion of one of Orlan's most important performances, 'The Kiss of the Artist/Le Baiser de l'artiste', from 1976-7.

Orlan's contribution to feminist ethics is an area few of her commentators have ventured into, but Malgorzata Lisiewicz's 1996 article 'Orlan: On the Border Between Ethics and Aesthetics' sets out the issues very clearly. Lisiewicz starts with the affirmation that 'traditional moral canons are also a product of the patriarchal system'; although Orlan's surgical work may have been tarred with the brush of madness or immorality, these are judgements made using the very ethical conventions that she is setting out to challenge. Much late twentieth-century art creates images that are not aesthetically pleasing, that provoke strong reactions in their viewers, and that make the viewer think about his/her understanding of what art is. The contemporary artistic climate, in other words, 'creates ethical images, instead of aesthetic ones' (Lisiewicz 1996: 48), and this is the context in which Orlan is operating:

> Her plastic surgeries are specific operations performed on the body of traditional ethics, which provokes the revision of so-far accepted moral notions. The body constitutes a peculiar cross-roads of contemporary discourses with the recognised law. In Orlan's case the junction point between the carnality and law creates an area saturated with tensions, where the confrontation of common morality and the ethics of "the other" occurs (Lisiewicz 1996: 48).

According to August Ruhs, Orlan 'has made ethics the very centre of her aesthetic programme', and 'women's sexual identity stands in the centre of this ethics' (Ruhs 1996: 154). The strength of Orlan's intervention in the field of ethics, though, is that it does not propose an alternative set of ethical rules or philosophical moral framework: '[s]he does not aim at another moral code nor the rigour of new rules' (ibid.). Rather than functioning as a set of moral rules, ethics, in Orlan's work, becomes 'less a specific technology than a specific technique of placing a subject within a social practice' – placing herself and her female body in the social and medical practice of cosmetic surgery, as a phenomenon it must come to terms with and try to explain. '[Ethics] becomes a technique of localising the subject "through" and placing it "in relation to the other"' (ibid.). Orlan's ethical self-positioning is feminist, not because it proposes alternative, woman-oriented ways of governing social behaviour and practices, but because it 'opposes a normative oppression of rules established by the [sic] man. This manifests itself in the insubordination to masculine canons of beauty and consequently, to the man-woman relation which determines the social order of roles' (ibid.: 51).

Orlan's aesthetics are ethical; they are also, and simultaneously, ethico-political. Orlan's conviction that art has political work to do rings through her explanatory discourse about her artistic career as well as through the performances themselves:

> Art that interests me has much in common with – belongs to – resistance. It must challenge our preconceptions, disrupt our thoughts; it is outside the norms, outside the law, against bourgeois order; it is not there to cradle us, to reinforce our comfort,

to serve up again what we already know. It must take risks, at the risk of not being immediately accepted or acceptable. It is deviant, and in itself a social project.[. . .] Too often we've seen in galleries that follow (even anticipate) institutional choice, very pretty products, neat and ready for sale, totally fabricated, empty and hollow; or at best clever! . . . well produced, nicely turned out. Art is not decoration for apartments, since we already have stuff for that: aquariums, plants, curtains and furniture. (Orlan 1996: 85)

This commitment to questioning established taste and norms, and to upturning the artistic status quo, was nowhere better demonstrated by Orlan than in her performance 'Le Baiser de l'Artiste', first done at the Caldas da Rainha Museum in Portugal in 1976, but repeated to its principal acclaim at the 1977 annual FIAC (Foire international d'art contemporain) at the Grand Palais in Paris. The work consisted of a photo sculpture of Orlan's naked torso, at throat level of which was written the instruction 'Insert 5F', with an arrow pointing to the nearby slot for coins. Participants in the performance watched their 5F coins fall down a transparent tube into a triangular see-through container attached at the sculpture's crotch. When the coin had descended, Orlan the real-life artist would leap from her nearby position to give the participant a kiss.

Orlan explains that this performance was playing out two texts she had written in collaboration with Hubert Besacier, 'Facing a Society of Mothers and Merchants', and 'Art and Prostitution'. Even without this illustrative function, the performance was obviously a direct comment on the laws of exchange and the circulation of commodities at work in the capitalist and consumerist art market. The commodity in Orlan's performance was her own body, a woman's body, and by deploying it in this way Orlan pointed up how the exchange of commodities in the art market functions in exactly the same way as the economics of prostitution, in which the woman's body is most often the commodity being paid for. Her exposure of the fundamentally similar economic dynamics of art and prostitution was nothing new in itself, as it has been a recurrent theme of artists since Baudelaire and the stage of modernity in which social and technological progress (essentially, mechanical reproduction) pushed artistic production into the marketplace. But 'Le Baiser de l'Artiste' revealed and performed the role of the woman's body in these economic processes as well as any other single work by a woman artist has done, and perhaps better.

Responses to Orlan's audacious commitment of her own body and its kisses to public economic exchange were interestingly varied; while women told her she was brave, brought her a glass of champagne, encouraged their (male) partner to come and try the experience, responded gently and erotically to

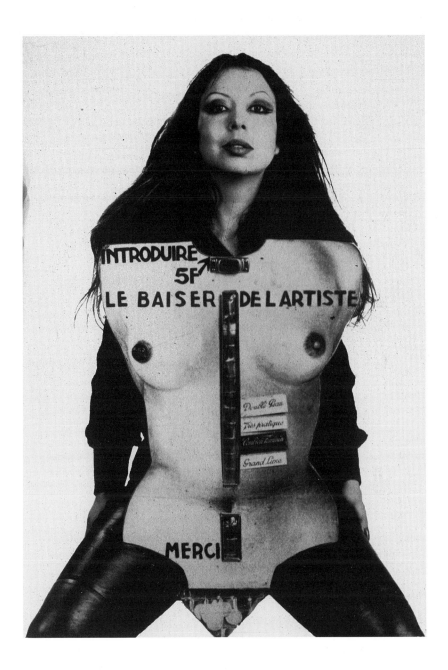

Figure 20. Baiser de l'artiste/The Kiss of the Artist, or automatic distribution, 5F performance at the FIAC, Paris, 1976. Black and white photo, 110cm × 170cm.

the kiss, and recoiled from Orlan's tongue inserting itself into her mouth, men tipped her in their own currency (100 schilling), were reluctant to pay and did not come up with the full 5F, came back several times, kissed the end of her nose in return, and incited other onlookers to take their turn.[4] Over the three days of the FIAC, about sixty people ventured their 5F (approximately twenty per day during the two to three hours Orlan directed the work), and according to Orlan people were attending just to see it by the third day, by which point she stopped the performance, as it was losing its 'surprise effect'.[5] The performance caused a considerable critical furore (reported by the French daily *Libération)* and led to Orlan's suspension from her teaching duties at the Atelier des Trois Soleils, for 'activities incompatible with her duties as an educator'.[6] Subsequently, forty-three of the forty-five students involved demonstrated in front of their class to demand her reinstatement.

The feminist theoretical text immediately brought to mind by 'Le Baiser de l'Artiste' is Luce Irigaray's 'When the Goods Get Together' ['Des marchandises entre elles'], published in the collection of essays *This Sex Which is Not One* in the same year as Orlan's performance, 1977. In this essay, where Irigaray emphasizes that the saturation of reality by consumption and commercialism is itself an attribute of the patriarchal system, she explains that the very male-dominated nature of trade (prostitution, in which women's bodies are effectively exchanged between pimp and client, is an extreme but relevant example) characterizes economic exchange as 'homosexual'. Masculine 'homosexuality', by which Irigaray means the not-usually-sexual social relationships between men (the term adopted in more recent theory has been 'homosocial') 'is the very basis of the general economy'. The assignment of roles in the economy is gendered through and through; 'some [men] are given the role of producing and exchanging subjects, while others [women] are assigned the role of productive earth and goods' (Marks and de Courtviron 1981: 107). Taking this argument one stage further, Irigaray asserts that women's role as 'goods', or objects of exchange, is at the basis of the entire economic system, since for as long as they are exchanged between men, it is impossible for women to take up the role of active exchanging subjects themselves. Conversely, men are 'traders only at the price of renouncing their function as goods' (ibid.: 108).

What Orlan's pay-and-kiss performance was critiquing above all else is the gendered, patriarchal and exploitative model of the capitalist economy,

---

4. Orlan and Stéphane Place (eds) (1997), *Orlan: de l'art charnel au baiser de l'artiste*, p. 54.
5. ibid., p. 55.
6. ibid., p. 52.

in which all exchanged objects are effectively 'prostituted', but women's bodies are at the bottom of the pile. Although she was only offering her clients kisses, not sexual relations, by effectively adopting the role of prostitute, Orlan took the risk of appearing complicit with the masculinist economic logic of capitalism. But what she was actually doing with her seeming complicity was miming patriarchal economic exchange precisely in order to expose and criticise it – a perfect example of the strategy of critical mimesis Irigaray suggests women avail themselves of in order to undermine and transform the functioning of patriarchal society (Whitford 1991: 71). Perhaps the most important aspect of 'Le Baiser de l'Artiste', though, was the most visible one, although one that it is oddly easy to overlook; the fact that the conceiver and performer of the work were identical with the person who stood to gain from it financially (if only to the tune of some 300F), Orlan herself. It was not possible for Orlan on her own to conduct the 'other' kind of trade that Irigaray says would exist if the goods got together – if there were an economic and social 'entre elles'. The notion of such an alternative economic system extending to French women's artistic production seems so far-fetched as to be laughable. But the predominantly generous and emotional (rather than financial) responses of Orlan's female clients suggest, as Irigaray does, that a feminine economy functions differently from a patriarchal 'homosexual' one, and that rather than being some utopian dream, it perhaps already exists in the interstices of our current masculinist capitalist modes of exchange. And if Orlan alone could not aspire in 1977 to the formation of 'a certain economy of abundance' (Marks and de Courtviron 1981: 110), it was nonetheless she, and she alone, who was in charge of the marketing of her own body.

The strategy of mimesis adopted by Orlan when she played the prostitute in 'Le Baiser de l'Artiste' might in fact be said to extend to many of her works and performances over the last thirty years. According to Irigaray's commentators, three types of feminine mimesis can be identified: straightforward 'parroting', which is not critical at all; a second level in which imitation turns into a 'masquerade', or a parody of patriarchal treatment of the feminine; and a third level in which miming familiar and stereotypical feminine roles 'signif[ies] difference as possibility', opening up a space for the performance of another kind of femininity (Whitford 1991: 205). Judith Butler's theory of gender performativity both accords with and develops Irigaray's notion that feminine identity is imitable and performable through and through, since Butler never ceases to emphasize that women's identity under patriarchy is constructed rather than given, made rather than found. What is made can be remade, performatively transformed into other formations of femaleness not yet known, and Orlan's performance art, pre-surgical and surgical, shows us this in fascinating and extreme ways.

Bibliography

Anzieu, Didier (1995), *Le Moi-peau*, Paris: Dunod (Bordas, 1985 pour la première édition).

Artaud, Antonin (1964), *Le théâtre et son double*, Paris: Gallimard 'Idées'.

Art Press International no. 5 (March 1977), 'Femmes-Différences'.

Art Press International no. 30 (July 1979), Special "Performances", 4–15.

Auslander, Philip (1989), 'Going with the Flow: Performance Art and Mass Culture', in *The Drama Review: a journal of performance studies*, Vol. 33 no. 2 (Summer 1989), 119–36.

Balsamo, Anne (1996), *Technologies of the Gendered Body: Reading Cyborg Women*, Durham and London: Duke University Press.

Barber, Stephen (1993), *Antonin Artaud: Blows and Bombs*, London: Faber & Faber.

Battersby, Christine (1993), 'Her Body/Her Boundaries: Gender and the Metaphysics of Containment', *Journal of Philosophy and the Visual Arts*, ed. Andrew Benjamin, 30–9.

Benjamin, Walter (1936), 'The Work of Art in the Age of Mechanical Reproduction', in *Illuminations*, ed. with introduction by Hannah Arendt, trans. Harry Zohn, London: Fontana Press, 1972, pp. 211–44.

Boothroyd, Dave (1996), 'Rewriting the Skin', paper given at the 'Sensual Writing' conference, University of Aberdeen, July 1996.

Bowlby, Rachel (1993), 'Frankenstein's woman-to-be: choice and the new reproductive technologies', in *Shopping with Freud*, London and New York: Routledge, pp. 82–93.

Braidotti, Rosi (1996a), *Nomadic Subjects: Embodiment and Sexual Difference in Contemporary Feminist Theory*, New York: Columbia University Press.

—— (1996b), 'Signs of Wonder and Traces of Doubt: on Teratology and Embodied Differences', in Nina Lykke and Rosi Braidotti (eds) (1996), *Between Monsters, Goddesses and Cyborgs: Feminist Confrontations with Science, Medicine and Cyberspace*, London and New Jersey: Zed Books, pp. 135–52.

—— (1996c), 'Mothers, Monsters, and Machines', in *Nomadic Subjects: Embodiment and Sexual Difference in Contemporary Feminist Theory*, New York: Columbia University Press, pp. 75–94.

Brand, Peggy Zeglin (1998), 'Disinterestedness and Political Art', in Carolyn Korsmeyer (ed.), *Aesthetics: the Big Questions*, Oxford: Basil Blackwell, pp. 155–71.

Bowie, Malcolm (1991), *Lacan*, London: Fontana Press.

Butler, Judith (1990), *Gender Trouble: Feminism and the Subversion of Identity*, London and New York: Routledge.

—— (1993), *Bodies that Matter: The Discursive Limits of 'Sex'*, London and New York: Routledge.

—— (1994), 'Gender as Performance: An Interview with Judith Butler', *Radical Philosophy* 67 (Summer 1994), 32–9.

Carlson, Marvin (1996), *Performance: A Critical Introduction*, London and New York: Routledge.

Cixous, Hélène and Clément, Catherine (1986), *The Newly Born Woman*, Minneapolis: University of Minnesota Press.

Clover, Carol (1992), 'The Eye of Horror', in *Men, Women and Chainsaws: Gender in the Modern Horror Film*, London: BFI Publishing.

Creed, Barbara (1993), *The Monstrous-Feminine: Film, Feminism, Psychoanalysis*, London and New York: Routledge.

Dallier-Poppier, Aline (ed.) (1982), 'Le mouvement des femmes dans l'art contemporain', (Colloque National Femmes, Féminisme, Recherches), Toulouse: University of Toulouse, 1982.

Davis, Kathy (1995), *Reshaping the Female Body: The Dilemma of Cosmetic Surgery*, London and New York: Routledge.

—— (1997), '"My Body is My Art": Cosmetic Surgery as Feminist Utopia?', in Kathy Davis, (ed.), *Embodied Practices: Feminist Perspectives on the Body*, London: SAGE Publications.

Deleuze, Gilles (1989), *Masochism*, trans. Jean McNeil, New York: Zone Books. Originally published as 'Le Froid et le Cruel', in *Présentation de Sacher-Masoch*, Paris: Editions de Minuit, 1967.

Deleuze, Gilles and Guattari, Félix (1986). *A Thousand Plateaus: capitalism and schizophrenia*, Minneapolis: University of Minnesota Press.

Erickson, Jon (1990), 'The Body as the Object of Modern Performance', *Journal of Dramatic Theory and Criticism* , Fall vol. 5 (1), 231–43.

Featherstone, Mike, and Burrows, Roger (1995), 'Cultures of Technological Embodiment: An Introduction', in Featherstone and Burrows (eds) (1995), *Cyberpunk/ Cyberspace/ Cyberbodies*, Theory, Culture & Society, London: SAGE Publications Ltd.

fémininmasculin: Le sexe de l'art, catalogue to exhibition held at Centre national d'art et de culture Georges Pompidou, 24 octobre 1995–12 février 1996, Paris: Editions du Centre Pompidou, 1995.

Féminisme, art et histoire de l'art, textes de Marcia Tucker, Lisa Tickner, Griselda Pollock, Rosi Huhn, Nicole Dubreuil-Blondin, Paris: Ecole nationale supérieure des Beaux-Arts, 1994.

Féral, Josette (1982), 'Performance and Theatricality: The Subject Demystified', *Modern Drama*, Vol. 25 no.1 (March 1982), 170–81.

Finley, Karen (1996), 'A Constant State of Becoming', interview by Richard Schechner in Carol Martin (ed), *A Sourcebook of Feminist Theatre and Performance*, London and New York: Routledge.

Fleck, Robert (1994), 'L'Actualité du Happening', in *Hors-Limites, l'art et la vie 1952-1994*, catalogue de l'exposition présentée du 9 novembre 1994 au 23 janvier 1995 au Centre national d'art et de culture Georges Pompidou, Paris: Editions du Centre Pompidou, 1994, pp. 310-19.

Frankel, Susannah (1997), 'Between the pleats', *Guardian* Weekend, 19 July 1997, pp. 14-19.

Freud, Sigmund (1922), 'Medusa's Head', *The Standard Edition of the Complete Psychological Works of Sigmund Freud*, Vol XVIII (1920-22), London: Hogarth Press, pp. 273-4.

Genette, Gérard (1994), *L'oeuvre d'art: transcendance et immanence*, Paris: Editions du Seuil.

George, David (1989), 'On Ambiguity: Towards a Post-Modern Performance Theory', *Theatre Research International*, Vol. 14 no.1 (Spring 1989), 71-85.

Goldberg, RoseLee (1995), *Performance Art: From Futurism to the Present*, London: Thames and Hudson, World Art Series.

Grant, Linda (1995), 'Written on the Body', *Guardian* Weekend, 1 April 1995, pp. 12-20.

Gray, Chris Hables (ed.) (1995), *The Cyborg Handbook*, London and New York: Routledge.

Groupes, Mouvements, Tendances de l'Art Contemporain depuis 1945, Paris: Ecole nationale supérieure des Beaux-Arts, 1989.

Grosz, Elizabeth (1990), *Jacques Lacan: A feminist introduction*, London and New York: Routledge.

Halberstam, Judith, and Livingston, Ira (1995), 'Introduction: Posthuman Bodies', in Halberstam, Judith and Livingston, Ira (eds) (1995), *Posthuman Bodies*, Bloomington and Indianapolis: Indiana University Press.

Haraway, Donna J. (1991), 'A Cyborg Manifesto: Science, Technology, and Socialist-Feminism in the Late Twentieth Century', in Donna Haraway, *Simians, Cyborgs and Women: The Reinvention of Nature*, London: Free Association Books.

—— (1992a), 'Ecce Homo, Ain't (Ar'n't) I a Woman, and Inappropriated Others: The Human in a Post-Humanist Landscape', in Judith Butler and Joan Scott (eds), *Feminists Theorize the Political*, London and New York: Routledge.

—— (1992b), 'The Promises of Monsters: A Regenerative Politics for Inappropriate/d Others', in Lawrence Grossberg, Cary Nelson and Paula Treichler (eds), *Cultural Studies*, London and New York: Routledge.

Hassan, Ihab (1980), 'The Question of Postmodernism', in Harry R Garvin (ed.) *Romanticism, Modernism, Postmodernism, Bucknell Review* special issue, vol. 25, pp. 117-26.

Hors-Limites, l'art et la vie 1952-1994, catalogue de l'exposition présentée du 9 novembre 1994 au 23 janvier 1995 au Centre national d'art et de culture Georges Pompidou, Paris: Editions du Centre Pompidou, 1994.

Irigaray, Luce (1984), 'La différence sexuelle', *Ethique de la différence sexuelle*, Paris: Editions de Minuit, pp. 13-25.

—— (1992), *J'aime a toi*, Paris: Editions Grasset & Fasquelle.

Kaplan, E. Ann (1993), 'Feminism(s)/Postmodernism(s): MTV and Alternate Women's Video and Performance Art', *Women and Performance: A Journal of Feminist Theory* vol. 6 (1 (11)), 55–76.

—— (1997), 'Body Politics: Menopause, Mastectomy and Cosmetic Surgery Films by Rainer, Tom and Onwurah', in E. Ann Kaplan, *Looking for the Other: Feminism, Film and the Imperial Gaze*, London: Routledge, 1997.

Kim, Sung Bok (1998), 'Is Fashion Art?', *Fashion Theory* Volume 2 Issue 1, 51–72.

Kosofsky Sedgwick, Eve, and Parker, Andrew (1995), *Performativity and Performance*, London and New York: Routledge.

Kristeva, Julia (1982), *Powers of Horror: An Essay on Abjection*, trans. Leon S. Roudiez, New York: Columbia University Press.

Labelle-Rojoux, Arnaud (1988), *L'acte pour l'art*, Paris: Les Editeurs Evidant.

Lacan, Jacques (1975), 'Dieu et la jouissance de La Femme', in *Le Séminaire. Livre XX*, 'Encore', Paris: Editions du Seuil, pp. 61–71.

—— (1977), *Ecrits: A Selection*, London: Tavistock.

La part des femmes dans l'art contemporain, catalogue to exhibition held at Centre d'animation culturelle, Ville de Vitry-sur-Seine, March 1984.

Laplanche, J. & Pontalis, J-B. (1973), *The Language of Psychoanalysis*, trans. D. Nicholson-Smith, London: Hogarth Press.

Lemoine-Luccioni, Eugénie (1983), *La robe: essai psychanalytique sur le vêtement*, Paris: Editions du Seuil.

Les Cahiers du GRIF no. 7 (June 1975), 'Les Femmes et l'art'.

Levinas, Emmanuel (1969), *Totality and Infinity: An Essay on Exteriority*, trans. by Alphonso Lingis, Martinus Nijhoff, The Hague.

—— (1981), *Otherwise than Being, or Beyond Essence,* trans. by Alphonso Lingis, Martinus Nijhoff, The Hague.

Lippard, Lucy (1976), 'The Pains and Pleasures of Rebirth: European and American Women's Body Art', in Lucy Lippard, *From the Center: Feminists' Essays on Women's Art,* New York: E.P. Dutton.

Lykke, Nina (1996a), 'Introduction', in *Between Monsters, Goddesses and Cyborgs: Feminist Confrontations with Science, Medicine and Cyberspace*, London and New Jersey: Zed Books, pp. 1–12.

—— (1996b), 'Between Monsters, Goddesses and Cyborgs: Feminist Confrontations with Science', in *Between Monsters, Goddesses and Cyborgs: Feminist Confrontations with Science, Medicine and Cyberspace*, London and New Jersey: Zed Books, pp. 13–29.

—— and Braidotti, Rosi (1996), *Between Monsters, Goddesses and Cyborgs: Feminist Confrontations with Science, Medicine and Cyberspace*, London and New Jersey: Zed Books.

Lyotard, Jean-François (1989), 'Can Thought go on without a Body?', in Andrew Benjamin (ed.), *The Lyotard Reader*, Oxford: Blackwell.

Manguel, Alberto (1997), *Bride of Frankenstein*, BFI Classics, London: BFI Publishing.

Marks, Elaine, and de Courtviron, Isabelle (eds) (1981), *New French Feminisms: an anthology*, Brighton, Sussex: The Harvester Press Ltd.

Martin, Carol (ed.) (1996), *A sourcebook of feminist theatre and performance*, London and New York: Routledge.

Meskimmon, Marsha (1996), *The Art of Reflection: Women Artists' Self-Portraiture in the Twentieth Century*, London: Scarlet Press.

Michaud, Yves (1994), 'Introduction', in *Féminisme, art et histoire de l'art*, Paris: Ecole nationale supérieure des Beaux-Arts, pp. 9–26.

Millet, Catherine (1994), *L'art contemporain en France*, Paris: Flammarion, 1987 & 1994.

—— (ed.) (1977), 'Femmes-Différences', numéro 5 d'Art Press International, mars 1977.

Moi, Toril (ed.) (1987), *French Feminist Thought: A Reader*, Oxford: Basil Blackwell, 1987.

Nead, Lynda (1992), *The Female Nude: art, sexuality and obscenity*, London: Routledge.

O'Dell, Kathy (1988), 'The Performance Artist as Masochist Woman', *Arts Magazine* Vol. 62 (Feb 1988), 96–8.

Pacteau, Francette (1994). *The Symptom of Beauty*, London: Reaktion Books.

Pane, Gina (1974), 'Lettre à une inconnue', *Artitudes international* no. 15/17 (October), Saint-Jeannet.

Parker, Andrew and Sedgwick, Eve Kosofsky (eds) (1995), 'Performativity and Performance', introduction to *Performativity and Performance*, London: Routledge, pp. 1–19.

Phelan, Peggy (1988), 'Feminist Theory, Poststructuralism and Performance', *The Drama Review: A Journal of Performance Studies*, Spring Vol. 32 (1) 107–27.

Pluchart, François (1975), *L'art corporel*, Paris: Editions Rodolphe Stadler.

Polhemus, Ted, and Randall, Housk (1996), *The Customized Body*, London and New York: Serpent's Tail.

Pontbriand, Chantal (1982), 'The eye finds no fixed point on which to rest . . .', *Modern Drama*, Vol. 25 no. 1 (March 1982), 154–62.

Premier Symposium International d'Art Performance de Lyon, Lyon: Editions du Cirque Divers, 1980.

Radford, Robert (1998), 'Dangerous Liaisons: Art, Fashion and Individualism', *Fashion Theory* Volume 2 Issue 2, 151–64.

Reik, Theodor (1975), *Of Love and Lust: On the Psychoanalysis of Romantic and Sexual Emotions*, London: Souvenir Press Ltd.

Rian, Jeff (1993), 'What's All This Body Art?', *Flash Art,* Vol. XXVI no. 168 (Jan/Feb 1993), 50–3.

Russo, Mary (1986), 'Female Grotesques: Carnival and Theory', in Teresa de Lauretis (ed.), *Feminist studies, critical studies*, Bloomington and Indianapolis: Indiana University Press.

Schneider, Rebecca (1996), *The Explicit Body in Performance,* London and New York: Routledge.

Schumacher, Claude (ed.) (1989), *Artaud on Theatre*, London: Methuen Drama, 1989.

Serres, Michel (1991), *Le Tiers-Instruit*, Paris: Gallimard, Collection Folio-Essais.

Shelley, Mary (1994), *Frankenstein*, the original 1818 text, ed. D.L. Macdonald and Kathleen Scherf, Ontario, Canada: Broadview Press Ltd.

Silverman, Kaja (1988), *The Acoustic Mirror: the Female Voice in Psychoanalysis and Cinema*, Bloomington and Indianapolis: Indiana University Press.

Simmel, Georg (1968), *The Conflict in Modern Culture and Other Essays*, trans. with intro. by K. Peter Etzkorn, New York: Teachers College Press.

—— (1985), 'Adornment', epigraph to Elizabeth Wilson, *Adorned in Dreams: Fashion and Modernity*, London: Virago Press.

Sobchack, Vivian (1995), 'Beating the Meat/Surviving the Text, or How to Get Out of This Century Alive', in Mike Featherstone and Roger Burrows (eds) (1995), *Cyberpunk/ Cyberspace/ Cyberbodies*, Theory, Culture & Society, London: SAGE Publications Ltd.

Sorcières no. 10 (July 1977), 'L'Art et les femmes', ed. Xavière Gauthier and Anne Rivière.

Tomas, David (1995), 'Feedback and Cybernetics: Reimaging the Body in the Age of Cybernetics', in Mike Featherstone and Roger Burrows (eds) (1995), *Cyberpunk/ Cyberspace/ Cyberbodies*, Theory, Culture & Society, London: SAGE Publications Ltd.

Whitford, Margaret (1991), *Luce Irigaray: Philosophy in the Feminine*, London and New York: Routledge.

Wilson, Emma (1999), 'Re-viewing Voyeurism: Performance and Vision (Kieslowski)' in Victoria Best and Peter Collier (eds), *Powerful Bodies: Performance in French Cultural Studies*, Bern: Peter Lang AG, pp. 73–82.

Wirth, Andrzej (1996), 'Beyond Benjamin: Performative Artwork and its Resistance to Reproduction', in Gerhard Fischer (ed.), *'With the Sharpened Axe of Reason': Approaches to Walter Benjamin*, Oxford, UK and Herndon, VA, USA: Berg, 1996.

Wright, Elizabeth (1984). *Psychoanalytic Criticism: Theory in Practice*, London and New York, Methuen.

Young, Iris Marion (1990), 'Throwing Like a Girl: A Phenomenology of Feminine Body Comportment, Motility and Spatiality', in Iris Marion Young, *Throwing Like a Girl and Other Essays in Feminist Philosophy and Social Theory*, Bloomington and Indianapolis: Indiana University Press.

Zizek, Slavoj (1991), 'Grimaces of the Real, or When the Phallus Appears', *October* 58 (Fall), 45–68.

Publications by and devoted solely to Orlan

Adams, Parveen (1994), 'This Is My Body', in *Suture – Phantasmen der Vollkommenheit*, Salzburg: Salzburger Kunstverein.

—— (1996), 'Operation Orlan', in *The Emptiness of the Image: Psychoanalysis and Sexual Difference*, London and New York: Routledge, pp. 141–59.

Armstrong, Rachel (1995), 'Post-Human Evolution', *Artifice* magazine, Issue 2, 52–63.

—— (1996), 'Carnal Art', unpublished leaflet distributed at Orlan's 1996 presentations.

Augsburg, Tanya (1998), 'Orlan's Performative Transformations of Subjectivity', in Peggy Phelan and Jill Lane (eds), *The Ends of Performance,* New York and London: New York University Press, pp. 285–314.

'Beauty and the I of the Beholder: A Conversation with Orlan', in *Border Crossings: A Magazine of the Arts,* Vol 17 No. 2 (May 1998), 44–7.

Beckett, Andy, 'Suffering for her Art', *Independent on Sunday,* 14 April 1996, pp. 18–21.

Brogowski, Leszek (1996), 'The Body as a Guarantee', *Magazyn Sztuki/Art Magazine Quarterly* No. 9, January 1996, 65–8.

Ceci est mon corps . . . ceci est mon logiciel/This is my body . . . this is my software, includes texts by Sarah Wilson, Michel Onfray, Allucquere Rosanne Stone, Serge François, Parveen Adams. Edited and produced by Duncan McCorquodale, Black Dog Publishing, 1996.

'Ceci est mon corps . . . ceci est mon logiciel . . . .Orlan', dossier on and interview with Orlan in *Art: Le Sabord: communication littéraire et visuelle* no. 49 (Spring/ Summer 1998), pp. 12–17.

Ceysson, Bernard (1990), 'Orlan, ultime chef-d'oeuvre', in 'Les Vingt ans de pub et de ciné de Saint Orlan', catalogue to exhibition held at Centre d'Art Contemporain de Basse-Normandie, Hérouville Saint-Clair, 28 September–10 November 1990, pp. 6–17.

Corner, Lena (1996), 'My face is my canvas – plastic surgery is my art', interview with Orlan in *The Big Issue,* 15–21 April 1996, p.10.

Desmons, Patrice (1991), 'Noms de Dieu!', in *VST: revue scientifique et culturelle de santé mentale* 23–24, sept.–déc 1991, 40–2.

Ermacora, Beate (1994), 'Orlan', *European Photography* 56 (1994), 15–19.

Esmeralda (1998), 'Orlan et l'élucidation de la chair', in 'art à contre corps', *quasimodo* no.5 (Spring 1998), 89–94.

Fabre, Gladys C. (1984), 'Femme sur les barricades, Orlan brandit le laser time', in exhibition catalogue to *Orlan: Skaï et Sky and Video,* galerie J. & J. Donguy, Paris, 6 novembre – 1er décembre 1984.

Gray, Louise (1996), 'Me, my surgeon and my art', *Guardian,* 2 April 1996, pp. 8–9.

Hirschorn, Michelle (1996), 'Orlan: artist in the post-human age of mechanical reincarnation: body as ready (to be re-) made', in Griselda Pollock (ed.), *Generations and Geographies in the Visual Arts: Feminist Readings,* London and New York: Routledge, 1996, pp. 110–34.

KS, 'Orlan: Penine Hart Gallery', *Art Forum* October 1993.

'Les Vingt ans de pub et de ciné de Saint Orlan', catalogue to exhibition held at Centre d'Art Contemporain de Basse-Normandie, Hérouville Saint-Clair, 28 September – 10 November 1990.

Lisiewicz, Malgorzata (1996), 'Orlan: On the Border Between Ethics and Aesthetics', *Magazyn Sztuki/Art Magazine Quarterly* No. 9 (January 1996), 47–51.

McClellan, Jim (1994), 'The Extensions of Woman', *Observer* 'Life' magazine, 17 April 1994, pp. 38–42.

Moos, Michael (1996), 'Memories of Being: Orlan's Theater of the Self', *Art + Text* 54, 67–72.

Onfray, Michel (1996), 'The Aesthetics of Surgery', in *Ceci est mon corps . . . ceci est mon logiciel/ This is my body . . . this is my software*, edited and produced by Duncan McCorquodale, London: Black Dog Publishing, pp. 30–9.

Orlan (1980), 'Orlan', in Jean Dupuy (ed.), *Collective Consciousness: Art Performances in the 70s*, New York: Performing Arts Journals, p. 228, trans. p. 203

Orlan (1995), '"I do not want to look like . . .": Orlan on becoming-Orlan', *Women's Art Magazine* No.64 (May/June 1995), 5–10.

Orlan (1996), 'Conférence', in *Ceci est mon corps . . . ceci est mon logiciel/This is my body . . . this is my software*, edited and produced by Duncan McCorquodale, London: Black Dog Publishing, pp. 81–93.

Orlan (1997), '"Carnal Art": Manifesto', inside front cover and pp. 2–3 in Orlan and Stéphane Place (eds), *Orlan: de l'art charnel au baiser de l'artiste*, Collection "Sujet Objet", Paris: Editions Jean-Michel Place.

Orlan (1998a), 'Surtout pas sage comme une image', in 'art à contre corps', *quasimodo* no.5 (Spring 1998), 95–101.

Orlan (1998b), 'Conférence' (updated version), in *Une oeuvre de Orlan*, textes de Marie-Josée Bataille, Christian Gattinoni, Bernard Lafargue, Orlan, Lydie Pearle, Isabelle Rieusset-Lemarié, Joël Savary, Collection Iconotexte, Marseilles: Editions Muntaner, pp. 49–80.

'Orlan: Painful Beauty of Transformation', dossier of 7 articles on Orlan, in Polish in *Magazyn Sztuki/Art Magazine Quarterly* No. 9 (January 1996), 18–68.

Orlan: Skaï et Sky and Video, catalogue of exhibition held at Galerie J & J Donguy, Paris, 6 novembre – 1er décembre 1984.

Orlan 1964–1996, testi di Achille Bonito Oliva, Bernard Ceysson, Bruno Di Marino, Vittorio Fagone, Ulla Karttunen, Mario Perniola, Roma: Diagonale s.r.l., 1996.

Orlan and Stéphane Place (eds), *Orlan: de l'art charnel au baiser de l'artiste*, Collection "Sujet Objet", Paris: Editions Jean-Michel Place, 1997.

Pollock, Griselda (1996), 'A Carnal Art? Orlan', *Portfolio* no. 23 (June 1996), 56–7.

Price, Anna (1995), 'Orlan', *Artifice* magazine, Issue 2, 44–51.

Rose, Barbara (1993), 'Is it Art? Orlan and the Transgressive Act', *Art in America* (February 1993), 82–7 and 125.

Ruhs, August (1996), 'Orlan: Orlan's metamorphoses', in catalogue of exhibition 'Kroppen som Membran/Body as Membrane', 12 January – 17 March 1996 at Kunsthallen Brandts Klaedefabrik, and June to August 1996 at the Nordic Arts Centre, Sveaborg, Finland, pp. 154–5.

Savary, Joël (1998), 'La Chirurgie et l'institution au chevet de la première opération de Sainte-Orlan', in *Une oeuvre de Orlan*, Collection Iconotexte, Marseilles: Editions Muntaner.

Stone, Rosanne Allucquere (1996), 'Speaking of the Medium: Marshall McLuhan Interviews', in *Ceci est mon corps . . . ceci est mon logiciel/This is my body . . . this is my software*, edited and produced by Duncan McCorqodale, London: Black Dog Publishing, pp. 42–51.

Une oeuvre de Orlan, textes de Marie-Josée Bataille, Christian Gattinoni, Bernard Lafargue, Orlan, Lydie Pearle, Isabelle Rieusset-Lemarié, Joël Savary, Collection Iconotexte, Marseilles: Editions Muntaner, 1998.

Utley, Alison (1996), 'Time to lock horns on the beauty debate', *The Times Higher Education Supplement*, 19 April 1996.

VST: revue scientifique et culturelle de santé mentale 23/24, sept.–déc 1991. This issue is devoted entirely to Orlan.

Wilson, Sarah (1995), 'Feminités-Mascarades', in *fémininmasculin: Le sexe de l'art*, catalogue to exhibition held at Centre national d'art et de culture Georges Pompidou, 24 octobre 1995 – 12 février 1996, Paris: Editions du Centre Pompidou, pp. 291–302.

—— (1996), 'L'histoire d'O, Sacred and Profane', in *Ceci est mon corps . . . ceci est mon logiciel/This is my body . . . this is my software*, edited and produced by Duncan McCorquodale, London: Black Dog Publishing, pp. 7–17 .

Films, Television, Radio and Internet

On Orlan

'Arena' on self-portraiture, BBC2, 1995.

'South Bank Show' on contemporary body artists (Ron Athey, Fakir Mustapha, Franko B., Orlan), London Weekend Television, 5/4/98.

'Kaleidoscope', BBC Radio 4, interview with Orlan 11/4/96.

Other

The Bride of Frankenstein, dir. James Whale, 1935.

Frankenstein: The True Story, dir. Jack Smight, 1973.

Metropolis, dir. Fritz Lang, 1926.

'Changing Faces', Channel 4 documentary series, September–October 1995.

'Tx' on technological artists, BBC 2, 30/12/95.

www.andam.culture.fr/andam/ laureats/scottf.html & www.papermag.com/stylin/ parisfall98/jeremy_scott/jeremy_scott.html
for material on Jeremy Scott.

www.walt.de/
for material on W&LT (Walter van Beirendonck).

Chronology of Orlan's Artistic Itinerary

Date	Performances, Events or Exhibitions (a selection)
1964–5	First performances in St-Etienne and Firminy, France include 'Les marches au ralenti' and Orlan's first street measuring.
1966–70	Action 'Les draps du trousseau souillures' performed in St-Etienne and Nice. 'Couture en clair obscure' ('Chiaroscuro sewing') exhibited at atelier Delaroa, St-Etienne (1968), also the location of *tableaux vivants* from 1969 to 1972.
1971	Action 'Je suis une homme et un femme', Toulouse.
1972	Measuring in 'Expo 63/42' at Maison de la Culture, St-Etienne.
1973–4	Further *tableaux vivants* in Lyon, and a street measuring in Avignon.
1975	'One-off striptease with trousseau sheets' at atelier Delaroa, Lyon; work in 'Triennale de la Peinture' at Maison de la Culture, St-Etienne.
1976	'Le Baiser de l'Artiste' ('The Kiss of the Artist') at Caldas da Rainha Museum, Portugal, and measurings in Strasbourg and Macon, France.
1977	'Le Baiser de l'Artiste' at FIAC (international contemporary art fair), Paris; represented at Espace Lyonnais d'Art Contemporain and N.R.A gallery, Paris.
1978	Measuring in international performance symposium at Musée St-Pierre, Lyon; 'Documentary Study. The Head of Medusa' at international performance symposium in Aachen (Aix-la-Chapelle), Germany; work at Lara Vincy gallery, Paris, and Ben Vautier's 'La différence' gallery, Nice.
1979	Unanticipated surgical operation-performance at international performance symposium in Lyon; Orlan makes her first public performance dressed as a Madonna at international body art festival at Centre Georges Pompidou, Paris.
1980	'Mise-en-scène for a saint' at Espace Lyonnais d'Art Contemporain; retrospective of measurings in Antwerp, Belgium; work at Centre Georges Pompidou, Paris and Musée d'Art Moderne de la ville de Paris.
1981	'Evénement Orlan' at Espace Lyonnais d'Art Contemporain; represented in exhibition 'The Self-Portrait' at Centre Georges Pompidou, at Ravenna Pinacothèque, Italy, Peccolo gallery, Livorno, Italy, Gn gallery,

Gdansk, Poland, and Gulbenkian Foundation selection from Paris Biennale, Portugal.

1982   'Panneaux d'affichage avenir publicité' (Publicity posters for virtual films) in Lyon; work at Espace 'Sixto/Notes', Milan, and Albi festival 'Future technology/future culture', France.

1983   Laser spectacle and giant projection of slides with music by Geneva opera orchestra, Geneva Festival; institutional measuring at the Guggenheim Museum, New York.

1984   'Mise-en-scène for an assumption' at J&J Donguy gallery, Paris; 'Mise en scène for a grand fiat' at Locarno festival, Switzerland.

1985   'Histoires Saintes de l'Art' ('Holy Art Histories/Stories') with Léa Lublin, Cergy-Pontoise, France; 'Metaphors of the Sacred' at F.A.C.L.I.M., Limoges, France; represented at 'Les immatériaux', Centre Georges Pompidou, Paris.

1986   Represented at video retrospective at Stedelijk Museum, Amsterdam; participation in Daniel Buren's 'Mouvements-recouvrements' via on-line arts network 'Art-Accès', Reims, France.

1987   Represented in 3rd Saintes festival of photography, Abbaye-aux-Dames, Saintes, France, and in 'Polyphonix 11' (international festival of poetry, music and performance) and 'Telematics and creation' at Centre Georges Pompidou, Paris.

1988–9   'Femmes cathodiques' at International Simone de Beauvoir Video Festival, Paris; 'La madone au minitel' ('The Madonna on the Minitel') at Palais de Tokyo, Paris; represented in Danaé Foundation's homage to Robert Filliou, Pouilly-en-Auxois, France, in Locarno video festival, Switzerland, and in 'Les transinteractifs' at MacLuhan Science Center, Toronto. Performance by satellite transmission between Toronto and Paris.

1990   Launch of surgical performance project 'The Reincarnation of Saint Orlan or Image New Image(s)', Newcastle, UK, 30 May. First operation-performance 'carnal art', 21 July, Paris. Second operation-performance 'the unicorn operation', 25 July, Paris. Third operation-performance, 11 September, Paris. Fourth operation-performance 'successful operation', with text of E. Lemoine-Luccioni's 'La robe', 8 December, Paris. 'Les 20 ans de pub et de ciné de Sainte Orlan', exhibition at Centre d'art contemporain de basse Normandie, Hérouville Saint-Clair, France; painting and video installation 'Le corps/le sacré', Carcassonne, France; represented at Biennial of innovative visual art Glasgow/London, UK.

1991   Fifth operation-performance 'Operation Opera', with text by Michel Serres, 6 July, Paris. Represented in 'Les couleurs de l'argent', Musée de la Poste, Paris.

1992   'Video installation for the ceiling' at Biennial of Contemporary Art, Sydney, Australia. Grant awarded for stay in India at Lallit Kala

Academy, Madras. Represented at Emily Harvey and Pat Hearn gallery, New York.

1993 Sixth operation-performance and multimedia exhibition 'Sacrifice', with text by Antonin Artaud, February, Liège, Belgium. Seventh operation-performance 'Omnipresence' at Sandra Gering gallery, New York, transmitted live by satellite to Centre Georges Pompidou, Paris, MacLuhan Centre, Toronto, Banff Multimedia Centre, Canada, 21 November (with exhibition at Sandra Gering gallery November-December). Eighth operation-performance, 8 December, New York. Ninth operation-performance, 14 December, New York. 'My flesh, the texts and the languages' exhibited at Penine Hart gallery, New York.

1994 Represented at 'Hors limites', Centre Georges Pompidou, Paris; in 'The Art of the French Portrait C19-C20' at the Shoto Museum of Art, Tokyo; in 'Fabricated Realities' (Ben, Stelarc, Orlan), Berlin; in 'Suture' by Salzburger Kunstverein, Salzburg, Austria; in 'The Body as Site' exhibition of performance-video, ICA, London; in 'French Art from '70 to '90' at Galleria d'arte moderna, Bologna, Italy; in Haines gallery exhibition of photography and video, San Francisco, USA.

1995 Represented at Centre Georges Pompidou retrospective of performance video, Paris; at 'Positionen zum ich', Kiel Kunsthalle, Germany; at 'Mirror gender roles and the historical significance of beauty', California College of Art, San Francisco; at Festival of New Technologies, University of Warwick, UK; at sculpture Biennial 'oltre de scultura', Padua, Italy; at Biennial of Contemporary Art and New Technologies, Lyon, France.

1996 Represented in 'Body as Membrane', Odense, Denmark; with 'This is my body . . . this is my software' at Zone gallery, Newcastle, UK and Portfolio gallery, Edinburgh, UK; with 'Woman with Head' in ICA 'Totally Wired' live arts festival, London; in 'is it art?' at Contemporary Arts Center, Cincinnati, USA and Katonah museum of art, Katonah, NY, USA; in 'L'art au corps' at Marseilles Museum of contemporary art, France; in 'Photokina' festival by Institut Français, Cologne, Germany; in 'Endurance' at Proton ICA, Amsterdam and Kulturhusset, Stockholm, Sweden; at 'fluctuations fugitives', Marne La Vallée, France; in SALA 1 retrospective and Studio Stéfania Miscetti, Rome, Italy; at the Contemporary Art Centre at the Nikolaj church, Copenhagen, Denmark.

1997 Represented at Biennial of contemporary art 'Unimplosive art exhibition', Venice, Italy; at art video exhibition at the Serpentine gallery, London; with 'This is my body...this is my software' at Camerawork gallery, London; in 'Le masque et le miroir' at the M.A.C.B.A Museum of contemporary and fine art, Barcelona, Spain; at the Galleria Lattuada, Milan, Italy; at 'Vraiment, féminisme et art' at Laura Cottingham gallery, Grenoble, France; with the CAPC colloquium 'Orlan, figure de la chimère' at University CRE3, Bordeaux, France; with police scientific

	services and the internet in 'Exogène. Principe d'extériorité', Copenhagen, Denmark; in 'Trash' at Trento Museum of contemporary art, Trento, Italy; in the Istanbul Biennial of contemporary art, Turkey; in 'Woman' at the Horsens Kunstmuseum, Denmark.
1998	Represented in M.A.K. 'Out of Actions: Between performance and the object 1949-79', Vienna, Austria and Los Angeles, USA; in 'l'Atelier' of Ecole Régionale des Beaux Arts de Nantes, France; in Sextus Contemporary Galleries 'L'art dégénéré II: des artistes contre l'extrême-droite'; in Reykjavik festival 'The human body' at the Living Art Museum, Reykjavik, Iceland'; at 'Fétiche-fétichisme', Galerie Passage de Retz, Paris; in 'Art Focus' at Chelouche Gallery, Tel Aviv, Israel.
1999	Touring exhibition 'Le sang, le coeur et le nid de l'aigle' starting at Musée Carillo Gil, Mexico, and going on to Monterey Museum of contemporary art (Mexico), Caracas (Colombia), Bogota (Venezuela), Rio de Janeiro, Sao Paulo (Brazil); represented at M.O.C.A, Tokyo, Japan; at 'Flesh', Jerusalem Museum of contemporary art, Israel; at 'Heavenly Figures', Düsseldorf Kunsthalle, Germany; at 'Année de la France', Reina Sofia Museum, Spain.

Index